Rebound

The Path to Home

By
Edgar A. Guest
Author of
"Just Folks" — 'Over Here"
"A Heap o Livin'"

The Reilly & Lee Co.
Chicago

The Path to Home

To
F. K. R.
A friend who had faith

INDEX

Index

Index

Index

The Path to Home

There's the mother at the doorway, and the chil-
    dren at the gate,
And the little parlor windows with the curtains
    white and straight.
There are shaggy asters blooming in the bed that
    lines the fence,
And the simplest of the blossoms seems of mighty
    consequence.
Oh, there isn't any mansion underneath God's
    starry dome
That can rest a weary pilgrim like the little place
    called home.

Men have sought for gold and silver; men have
    dreamed at night of fame;
In the heat of youth they've struggled for achieve-
    ment's honored name;
But the selfish crowns are tinsel, and their shining
    jewels paste,
And the wine of pomp and glory soon grows
    bitter to the taste.
For there's never any laughter, howsoever far
    you roam,
Like the laughter of the loved ones in the happi-
    ness of home.

There is nothing so important as the mother's
    lullabies,
Filled with peace and sweet contentment, when
    the moon begins to rise —
Nothing real except the beauty and the calm upon
    her face
And the shouting of the children as they scamper
    round the place.
For the greatest of man's duties is to keep his
    loved ones glad
And to have his children glory in the father they
    have had.

So where'er a man may wander, and whatever be
    his care,
You'll find his soul still stretching to the home
    he left somewhere.
You'll find his dreams all tangled up with holly-
    hocks in bloom,
And the feet of little children that go racing
    through a room,
With the happy mother smiling as she watches
    them at play —
These are all in life that matter, when you've
    stripped the sham away.

The Path to Home

There's the mother at the doorway, and the children at the gate,
And the little parlor windows with the curtains
white and straight.
There are shaggy asters blooming in the bed that
lines the fence,
And the simplest of the blossoms seems of mighty
consequence.
Oh, there isn't any mansion underneath God's
starry dome
That can rest a weary pilgrim like the little place
called home.

Men have sought for gold and silver; men have
dreamed at night of fame;
In the heat of youth they've struggled for achieve-
ment's honored name;
But the selfish crowns are tinsel, and their shining
jewels paste,
And the wine of pomp and glory soon grows
bitter to the taste.
For there's never any laughter, howsoever far
you roam,
Like the laughter of the loved ones in the happiness of home.

There is nothing so important as the mother's
lullabies,
Filled with peace and sweet contentment, when
the moon begins to rise —
Nothing real except the beauty and the calm upon
her face
And the shouting of the children as they scamper
round the place.
For the greatest of man's duties is to keep his
loved ones glad
And to have his children glory in the father they
have had.

So where'er a man may wander, and whatever be
his care,
You'll find his soul still stretching to the home
he left somewhere.
You'll find his dreams all tangled up with holly-
hocks in bloom,
And the feet of little children that go racing
through a room,
With the happy mother smiling as she watches
them at play —
These are all in life that matter, when you've
stripped the sham away.

Fine

Isn't it fine when the day is done,
And the petty battles are lost or won,
When the gold is made and the ink is dried,
To quit the struggle and turn aside
To spend an hour with your boy in play,
And let him race all of your cares away?

Isn't it fine when the day's gone well,
When you have glorious tales to tell,
And your heart is light and your head is high.
For nothing has happened to make you sigh,
To hurry homewards to share the joy
That your work has won with a little boy?

Isn't it fine, whether good or bad
Has come to the hopes and the plans you had,
And the day is over, to find him there,
Thinking you splendid and just and fair,
Ready to chase all your griefs away,
And soothe your soul with an hour of play?

Oh, whether the day's been long or brief,
Whether it's brought to me joy or grief,
Whether I've failed, or whether I've won,
It shall matter not when the work is done;
I shall count it fine if I end each day
With a little boy in an hour of play.

Spoiling Them

" You're spoiling them!" the mother cries
When I give way to weepy eyes
And let them do the things they wish,
Like cleaning up the jelly dish,
Or finishing the chocolate cake,
Or maybe let the rascal take
My piece of huckleberry pie,
Because he wants it more than I.

" You're spoiling them!" the mother tells,
When I am heedless to their yells,
And let them race and romp about
And do not put their joy to rout.
I know I should be firm, and yet
I tried it once to my regret;
I will remember till I'm old
The day I started in to scold.

I stamped my foot and shouted: " Stop!"
And Bud just let his drum sticks drop,
And looked at me, and turned away;
That night there was no further play.
The girls were solemn-like and still,
Just as girls are when they are ill,
And when unto his cot I crept,
I found him sobbing as he slept.

That was my first attempt and last
To play the scold. I'm glad it passed
So quickly and has left no trace
Of memory on each little face;
But now when mother whispers low:
"You're spoiling them," I answer, "No!
But it is plain, as plain can be,
Those little tykes are spoiling me."

An Old-Fashioned Welcome

There's nothing cheers a fellow up just like a
    hearty greeting,
A handclasp and an honest smile that flash the
    joy of meeting;
And when at friendly doors you ring, somehow
    it seems to free you
From all life's doubts to hear them say: " Come
    in! We're glad to see you!"

At first the portal slips ajar in answer to your
    ringing,
And then your eyes meet friendly eyes, and wide
    the door goes flinging;
And something seems to stir the soul, however
    troubled be you,
If but the cheery host exclaims: "Come in!
    We're glad to see you!"

Our House

We play at our house and have all sorts of fun,
An' there's always a game when the supper is
    done;
An' at our house there's marks on the walls an'
    the stairs,
An' some terrible scratches on some of the chairs;
An' ma says that our house is really a fright,
But pa and I say that our house is all right.

At our house we laugh an' we sing an' we shout,
An' whirl all the chairs an' the tables about,
An' I rassle my pa an' I get him down too,
An' he's all out of breath when the fightin' is
    through;
An' ma says that our house is surely a sight,
But pa an' I say that our house is all right.

I've been to houses with pa where I had
To sit in a chair like a good little lad,
An' there wasn't a mark on the walls an' the
    chairs,
An' the stuff that we have couldn't come up to
    theirs;
An' pa said to ma that for all of their joy
He wouldn't change places an' give up his boy.

They never have races nor rassles nor fights,
Coz they have no children to play with at nights;
An' their walls are all clean an' their curtains
      hang straight,
An' everything's shiny an' right up to date;
But pa says with all of its racket an' fuss,
He'd rather by far live at our house with us.

A Plea

God grant me these: the strength to do
   Some needed service here;
The wisdom to be brave and true;
   The gift of vision clear,
That in each task that comes to me
Some purpose I may plainly see.

God teach me to believe that I
   Am stationed at a post,
Although the humblest 'neath the sky,
   Where I am needed most.
And that, at last, if I do well
My humble services will tell.

God grant me faith to stand on guard,
   Uncheered, unspoke, alone,
And see behind such duty hard
   My service to the throne.
Whate'er my task, be this my creed:
I am on earth to fill a need.

"Tell us a story," comes the cry
   From little lips when nights are cold,
And in the grate the flames leap high.
   "Tell us a tale of pirates bold,
Or fairies hiding in the glen,
   Or of a ship that's wrecked at sea."
I fill my pipe, and there and then
   Gather the children round my knee.

I give them all a role to play —
   No longer are they youngsters small,
And I, their daddy, turning gray;
   We are adventurers, one and all.
We journey forth as Robin Hood
   In search of treasure, or to do
Some deed of daring or of good;
   Our hearts are ever brave and true.

We take a solemn oath to be
   Defenders of the starry flag;
We brave the winter's stormy sea,
   Or climb the rugged mountain crag,
To battle to the death with those
   Who would defame our native land;
We pitch our camp among the snows
   Or on the tropics' burning sand.

We rescue maidens, young and fair,
  Held captive long in prison towers;
We slay the villain in his lair,
  For we're possessed of magic powers.
And though we desperately fight,
  When by our foes are we beset,
We always triumph for the right;
  We have not lost a battle yet.

It matters not how far we stray,
  Nor where our battle lines may be,
We never get so far away
  That we must spend a night at sea.
It matters not how high we climb,
  How many foes our pathway block,
We always conquer just in time
  To go to bed at 9 o'clock.

The Mother Watch

She never closed her eyes in sleep till we were
    all in bed;
On party nights till we came home she often sat
    and read.
We little thought about it then, when we were
    young and gay,
How much the mother worried when we children
    were away.
We only knew she never slept when we were out
    at night,
And that she waited just to know that we'd come
    home all right.

Why, sometimes when we'd stayed away till one
    or two or three,
It seemed to us that mother heard the turning
    of the key;
For always when we stepped inside she'd call
    and we'd reply,
But we were all too young back then to under-
    stand just why.
Until the last one had returned she always kept
    a light,
For mother couldn't sleep until she'd kissed us
    all good night.

She had to know that we were safe before she
       went to rest;
She seemed to fear the world might harm the
       ones she loved the best.
And once she said: " When you are grown to
       women and to men,
Perhaps I'll sleep the whole night through; I may
       be different then."
And so it seemed that night and day we knew a
       mother's care —
That always when we got back home we'd find
       her waiting there.

Then came the night that we were called to gather
       round her bed:
" The children all are with you now," the kindly
       doctor said.
And in her eyes there gleamed again the old-time
       tender light
That told she had been waiting just to know we
       were all right.
She smiled the old-familiar smile, and prayed to
       God to keep
Us safe from harm throughout the years, and
       then she went to sleep.

Faces

I look into the faces of the people passing by,
  The glad ones and the sad ones, and the lined
    with misery,
And I wonder why the sorrow or the twinkle in
    the eye;
  But the pale and weary faces are the ones that
    trouble me.

I saw a face this morning, and time was when it
    was fair;
  Youth had brushed it bright with color in the
    distant long ago,
And the goddess of the lovely once had kept a
    temple there,
  But the cheeks were pale with grieving and
    the eyes were dull with woe.

Who has done this thing I wondered; what has
    wrought the ruin here?
  Why these sunken cheeks and pallid where the
    roses once were pink?
Why has beauty fled her palace; did some vandal
    hand appear?
  Did her lover prove unfaithful or her husband
    take to drink?

Once the golden voice of promise whispered
    sweetly in her ears;
  She was born to be a garden where the smiles
    of love might lurk;
Now the eyes that shone like jewels are but gate-
    ways for her tears,
  And she takes her place among us, toilers early
    bound for work.

Is it fate that writes so sadly, or the cruelty of
    man?
  What foul deed has marred the parchment of
    a life so fair as this?
Who has wrecked this lovely temple and de-
    stroyed the Maker's plan,
  Raining blows on cheeks of beauty God had
    fashioned just to kiss?

Oh, the pale and weary faces of the people that
    I see
  Are the ones that seem to haunt me, and I
    pray to God above
That such cruel desolation shall not ever come
    to be
  Stamped forever in the future on the faces
    that I love.

The Lost Purse

I remember the excitement and the terrible alarm
That worried everybody when William broke
his arm;
An' how frantic Pa and Ma got only jes' the
other day
When they couldn't find the baby coz he'd up
an' walked away;
But I'm sure there's no excitement that our house
has ever shook
Like the times Ma can't remember where she's
put her pocketbook.

When the laundry man is standin' at the door an'
wants his pay
Ma hurries in to get it, an' the fun starts right
away.
She hustles to the sideboard, coz she knows
exactly where
She can put her hand right on it, but alas! it isn't
there.
She tries the parlor table an' she goes upstairs
to look,
An' once more she can't remember where she put
her pocketbook.

She tells us that she had it just a half an hour
ago

24

An' now she cannot find it though she's hunted
    high and low;
She's searched the kitchen cupboard an' the
    bureau drawers upstairs,
An' it's not behind the sofa nor beneath the par-
    lor chairs.
She makes us kids get busy searching every little
    nook,
An' this time says she's certain that she's lost
    her pocketbook.

She calls Pa at the office an' he laughs I guess,
    for then
She always mumbles something 'bout the heart-
    lessness of men.
She calls to mind a peddler who came to the
    kitchen door,
An' she's certain from his whiskers an' the
    shabby clothes he wore
An' his dirty shirt an' collar that he must have
    been a crook,
An' she's positive that feller came and got her
    pocketbook.

But at last she allus finds it in some queer an'
    funny spot,
Where she'd put it in a hurry, an' had somehow
    clean forgot;

An' she heaves a sigh of gladness, an' she says,
  " Well, I declare,
I would take an oath this minute that I never put
  it there."
An' we're peaceable an' quiet till next time Ma
  goes to look
An' finds she can't remember where she put her
  pocketbook.

The Doctor

I don't see why Pa likes him so,
  And seems so glad to have him come;
He jabs my ribs and wants to know
  If here and there it's hurting some.
He holds my wrist, coz there are things
  In there, which always jump and jerk,
Then, with a telephone he brings,
  He listens to my breather work.

He taps my back and pinches me,
  Then hangs a mirror on his head
And looks into my throat to see
  What makes it hurt and if it's red.
Then on his knee he starts to write
  And says to mother, with a smile:
" This ought to fix him up all right,
  We'll cure him in a little while."

I don't see why Pa likes him so.
    Whenever I don't want to play
He says: "The boy is sick, I know!
    Let's get the doctor right away."
And when he comes, he shakes his hand,
    And hustles him upstairs to me,
And seems contented just to stand
    Inside the room where he can see.

Then Pa says every time he goes:
    "That's money I am glad to pay;
It's worth it, when a fellow knows
    His pal will soon be up to play."
But maybe if my Pa were me,
    And had to take his pills and all,
He wouldn't be so glad to see
    The doctor come to make a call.

Lines For a Flag Raising Ceremony

Full many a flag the breeze has kissed;
  Through ages long the morning sun
Has risen o'er the early mist
  The flags of men to look upon.
And some were red against the sky,
  And some with colors true were gay,
And some in shame were born to die,
  For Flags of hate must pass away.
Such symbols fall as men depart,
  Brief is the reign of arrant might;
The vicious and the vile at heart
  Give way in time before the right.

A flag is nothing in itself;
  It but reflects the lives of men;
And they who lived and toiled for pelf
  Went out as vipers in a den.
God cleans the sky from time to time
  Of every tyrant flag that flies,
And every brazen badge of crime
  Falls to the ground and swiftly dies.
Proud kings are mouldering in the dust;
  Proud flags of ages past are gone;
Only the symbols of the just
  Have lived and shall keep living on.

So long as we shall serve the truth,
  So long as honor stamps us fair,
Each age shall pass unto its youth
  Old Glory proudly flying there!
But if we fail our splendid past,
  If we prove faithless, weak and base,
That age shall be our banner's last;
  A fairer flag shall take its place.
This flag we fling unto the skies
  Is but an emblem of our hearts,
And when our love of freedom dies,
  Our banner with our race departs.

Full many a flag the breezes kiss,
  Full many a flag the sun has known,
But none so bright and fair as this;
  None quite so splendid as our own!
This tells the world that we are men
  Who cling to manhood's ways and truth;
It is our soul's great voice and pen,
  The strength of age, the guide of youth,
And it shall ever hold the sky
  So long as we shall keep our trust;
But if our love of right shall die
  Our Flag shall sink into the dust.

The Toy-Strewn Home

Give me the house where the toys are strewn,
  Where the dolls are asleep in the chairs,
Where the building blocks and the toy balloon
  And the soldiers guard the stairs.
Let me step in a house where the tiny cart
  With the horses rules the floor,
And rest comes into my weary heart,
  For I am at home once more.

Give me the house with the toys about,
  With the battered old train of cars,
The box of paints and the books left out,
  And the ship with her broken spars.
Let me step in a house at the close of day
  That is littered with children's toys,
And dwell once more in the haunts of play,
  With the echoes of by-gone noise.

Give me the house where the toys are seen,
  The house where the children romp,
And I'll happier be than man has been
  'Neath the gilded dome of pomp.
Let me see the litter of bright-eyed play
  Strewn over the parlor floor,
And the joys I knew in a far-off day
  Will gladden my heart once more.

Whoever has lived in a toy-strewn home,

Though feeble he be and gray,
Will yearn, no matter how far he roam,
  For the glorious disarray
Of the little home with its littered floor
  That was his in the by-gone days;
And his heart will throb as it throbbed before,
  When he rests where a baby plays.

Kindness

One never knows
How far a word of kindness goes;
One never sees
How far a smile of friendship flees.
Down, through the years,
The deed forgotten reappears.

One kindly word
The souls of many here has stirred.
Man goes his way
And tells with every passing day,
Until life's end:
" Once unto me he played the friend."

We cannot say
What lips are praising us to-day.
We cannot tell
Whose prayers ask God to guard us well.
But kindness lives
Beyond the memory of him who gives.

Under the Roof Where the Laughter Rings

Under the roof where the laughter rings,
    That's where I long to be;
There are all of the glorious things,
    Meaning so much to me.
There is where striving and toiling ends;
There is where always the rainbow bends.

Under the roof where the children shout,
    There is the perfect rest;
There is the clamor of greed shut out,
    Ended the ceaseless quest.
Battles I fight through the heat of to-day
Are only to add to their hours of play.

Under the roof where the eyes are bright,
    There I would build my fame;
There my record of life I'd write;
    There I would sign my name.
There in laughter and true content
Let me fashion my monument.

Under the roof where the hearts are true,
    There is my earthly goal;
There I am pledged till my work is through,
    Body and heart and soul.
Think you that God will my choice condemn
If I have never played false to them?

St. Valentine's Day

Let loose the sails of love and let them fill
  With breezes sweet with tenderness to-day;
  Scorn not the praises youthful lovers say;
Romance is old, but it is lovely still.
  Not he who shows his love deserves the jeer,
  But he who speaks not what she longs to hear.

There is no shame in love's devoted speech;
  Man need not blush his tenderness to show;
  'Tis shame to love and never let her know,
To keep his heart forever out of reach.
  Not he the fool who lets his love go on,
  But he who spurns it when his love is won.

Men proudly vaunt their love of gold and fame,
  High station and accomplishments of skill,
  Yet of life's greatest conquest they are still,
And deem it weakness, or an act of shame,
  To seem to place high value on the love
  Which first of all they should be proudest of.

Let loose the sails of love and let them take
  The tender breezes till the day be spent;
  Only the fool chokes out life's sentiment.
She is a prize too lovely to forsake.
  Be not ashamed to send your valentine;
  She has your love, but needs its outward sign.

Dr. Johnson's Picture Cow

Got a sliver in my hand
An' it hurt t' beat the band,
An' got white around it, too;
Then the first thing that I knew
It was all swelled up, an' Pa
Said: "There's no use fussin', Ma,
Jes' put on his coat an' hat;
Doctor Johnson must see that."

I was scared an' yelled, because
One time when the doctor was
At our house he made me smell
Something funny, an' I fell
Fast asleep, an' when I woke
Seemed like I was goin' t' choke;
An' the folks who stood about
Said I'd had my tonsils out.

An' my throat felt awful sore
An' I couldn't eat no more,
An' it hurt me when I'd talk,
An' they wouldn't let me walk.
So when Pa said I must go
To the doctor's, I said: "No,
I don't want to go to-night,
'Cause my hand will be all right."

Pa said: " Take him, Ma," an' so
I jes' knew I had t' go.
An' the doctor looked an' said:
" It is very sore an' red —
Much too sore to touch at all.
See that picture on the wall,
That one over yonder, Bud,
With the old cow in the mud?

" Once I owned a cow like that,
Jes' as brown an' big an' fat,
An' one day I pulled her tail
An' she kicked an' knocked the pail
Full o' milk clean over me."
Then I looked up there t' see
His old cow above the couch,
An' right then I hollered 'ouch.' "

" Bud," says he, " what's wrong with you;
Did the old cow kick you, too?"
An' he laughed, an' Ma said: " Son,
Never mind, now, it's all done."
Pretty soon we came away
An' my hand's all well to-day.
But that's first time that I knew
Picture cows could kick at you.

Compensation

I'd like to think when life is done
   That I had filled a needed post,
That here and there I'd paid my fare
   With more than idle talk and boast;
That I had taken gifts divine,
The breath of life and manhood fine,
And tried to use them now and then
In service for my fellow men.

I'd hate to think when life is through
   That I had lived my round of years
A useless kind, that leaves behind
   No record in this vale of tears;
That I had wasted all my days
By treading only selfish ways,
And that this world would be the same
If it had never known my name.

I'd like to think that here and there,
   When I am gone, there shall remain
A happier spot that might have not
   Existed had I toiled for gain;
That some one's cheery voice and smile
Shall prove that I had been worth while;
That I had paid with something fine
My debt to God for life divine.

It Couldn't Be Done

Somebody said that it couldn't be done,
   But he with a chuckle replied
That " maybe it couldn't," but he would be one
   Who wouldn't say so till he'd tried.
So he buckled right in with the trace of a grin
   On his face. If he worried he hid it.
He started to sing as he tackled the thing
   That couldn't be done, and he did it.

Somebody scoffed: "Oh, you'll never do that;
   At least no one ever has done it";
But he took off his coat and he took off his hat,
   And the first thing we knew he'd begun it.
With a lift of his chin and a bit of a grin,
   Without any doubting or quiddit,
He started to sing as he tackled the thing
   That couldn't be done, and he did it.

There are thousands to tell you it cannot be done,
   There are thousands to prophesy failure;
There are thousands to point out to you one by
      one,
   The dangers that wait to assail you.
But just buckle in with a bit of a grin,
   Just take off your coat and go to it;
Just start in to sing as you tackle the thing
   That " cannot be done," and you'll do it.

Service

You never hear the robins brag about the sweet-
      ness of their song,
Nor do they stop their music gay whene'er a
      poor man comes along.
God taught them how to sing an' when they'd
      learned the art He sent them here
To use their talents day by day the dreary lives
      o' men to cheer.
An' rich or poor an' sad or gay, the ugly an'
      the fair to see,
Can stop most any time in June an' hear the
      robins' melody.

I stand an' watch them in the sun, usin' their
      gifts from day to day,
Swellin' their little throats with song, regardless
      of man's praise or pay:
Jes' bein' robins, nothing else, nor claiming great-
      ness for their deeds,
But jes' content to gratify one of the big world's
      many needs,
Singin' a lesson to us all to be ourselves and
      scatter cheer
By usin' every day the gifts God gave us when
      He sent us here.

Why should we keep our talents hid, or think
    we favor men because
We use the gifts that God has given? The
    robins never ask applause,
Nor count themselves remarkable, nor strut in a
    superior way,
Because their music sweeter is than that God
    gave unto the jay.
Only a man conceited grows as he makes use of
    talents fine,
Forgetting that he merely does the working of
    the Will Divine.

Lord, as the robins, let me serve! Teach me to
    do the best I can
To make this world a better place, an' happier
    for my fellow man.
If gift o' mine can cheer his soul an' hearten him
    along his way
Let me not keep that talent hid; I would make
    use of it to-day.
An' since the robins ask no praise, or pay for all
    their songs o' cheer,
Let me in humbleness rejoice to do my bit o'
    service here.

At the Peace Table

Who shall sit at the table, then, when the terms
    of peace are made —
The wisest men of the troubled lands in their
    silver and gold brocade?
Yes, they shall gather in solemn state to speak
    for each living race,
But who shall speak for the unseen dead that shall
    come to the council place?

Though you see them not and you hear them not,
    they shall sit at the table, too;
They shall throng the room where the peace is
    made and know what it is you do;
The innocent dead from the sea shall rise to stand
    at the wise man's side,
And over his shoulder a boy shall look — a boy
    that was crucified.

You may guard the doors of that council hall with
    barriers strong and stout,
But the dead unbidden shall enter there, and never
    you'll shut them out.
And the man that died in the open boat, and the
    babes that suffered worse,
Shall sit at the table when peace is made by the
    side of a martyred nurse.

You may see them not, but they'll all be there;
    when they speak you may fail to hear;
You may think that you're making your pacts
    alone, but their spirits will hover near;
And whatever the terms of the peace you make
    with the tyrant whose hands are red,
You must please not only the living here, but must
    satisfy your dead.

Mrs. Malone and the Censor

When Mrs. Malone got a letter from Pat
She started to read it aloud in her flat.
"Dear Mary," it started, "I can't tell you much,
I'm somewhere in France, and I'm fightin' the
    Dutch;
I'm chokin' wid news thot I'd like to relate,
But it's little a soldier's permitted t' state.
Do ye mind Red McPhee — well, he fell in a
    ditch
An' busted an arrm, but I can't tell ye which.

"An' Paddy O'Hara was caught in a flame
An' rescued by — Faith, I can't tell ye his name.
Last night I woke up wid a terrible pain;
I thought for awhile it would drive me insane.
Oh, the suff'rin, I had was most dreadful t' bear!

41

I'm sorry, my dear, but I can't tell ye where.
The doctor he gave me a pill, but I find
It's conthrary to rules t' disclose here the kind.

" I've been t' the dintist an' had a tooth out.
I'm sorry t' leave you so shrouded in doubt
But the best I can say is that one tooth is gone,
The censor won't let me inform ye which one.
I met a young fellow who knows ye right well,
An' ye know him, too, but his name I can't tell.
He's Irish, red-headed, an' there with th' blarney,
His folks once knew your folks back home in
        Killarney."

" By gorry," said Mrs. Malone in her flat,
" It's hard t' make sinse out av writin' like that,
But I'll give him as good as he sends, that I will."
So she went right to work with her ink well an'
        quill,
An' she wrote, " I suppose ye're dead eager fer
        news —
You know when ye left we were buyin' the shoes;
Well, the baby has come, an' we're both doin'
        well;
It's a ———. Oh, but that's somethin' they won't
        let me tell."

The Unknown Friends

We cannot count our friends, nor say
How many praise us day by day.
   Each one of us has friends that he
   Has yet to meet and really know,
   Who guard him, wheresoe'er they be,
   From harm and slander's cruel blow.
They help to light our path with cheer,
Although they pass as strangers here.

These friends, unseen, unheard, unknown,
Our lasting gratitude should own.
   They serve us in a thousand ways
   Where we perhaps should friendless be;
   They tell our worth and speak our praise
   And for their service ask no fee;
They choose to be our friends, although
We have not learned to call them so.

We cannot guess how large the debt
We owe to friends we have not met.
   We only know, from day to day,
   That we discover here and there
   How one has tried to smooth our way,
   And ease our heavy load of care,
Then passed along and left behind
His friendly gift for us to find.

First Name Friends

Though some may yearn for titles great, and
      seek the frills of fame,
I do not care to have an extra handle to my name.
I am not hungry for the pomp of life's high
      dignities,
I do not sigh to sit among the honored LL. D.'s.
I shall be satisfied if I can be unto the end,
To those I know and live with here, a simple,
      first-name friend.

There's nothing like the comradeship which
      warms the lives of those
Who make the glorious circle of the Jacks and
      Bills and Joes.
With all his majesty and power, Old Caesar never
      knew
The joy of first-name fellowship, as all the
      Eddies do.
Let them who will be "mistered" here and raised
      above the rest;
I hold a first-name greeting is by far the very
      best.

Acquaintance calls for dignity. You never really
      know
The man on whom the terms of pomp you feel
      you must bestow.

Professor William Joseph Wise may be your
　　　friend, but still
You are not certain of the fact till you can call
　　　him Bill.
But hearts grow warm and lips grow kind, and
　　　all the shamming ends,
When you are in the company of good old first-
　　　name friends.

The happiest men on earth are not the men of
　　　highest rank;
That joy belongs to George, and Jim, to Henry
　　　and to Frank;
With them the prejudice of race and creed and
　　　wealth depart,
And men are one in fellowship and always light
　　　of heart.
So I would live and laugh and love until my sun
　　　descends,
And share the joyous comradeship of honest
　　　first-name friends.

The Furnace Door

My father is a peaceful man;
He tries in every way he can
To live a life of gentleness
And patience all the while.
He says that needless fretting's vain,
That it's absurd to be profane,
That nearly every wrong can be
Adjusted with a smile.
Yet try no matter how he will,
There's one thing that annoys him still,
One thing that robs him of his calm
And leaves him very sore;
He cannot keep his self-control
When with a shovel full of coal
He misses where it's headed for,
And hits the furnace door.

He measures with a careful eye
The space for which he's soon to try,
Then grabs his trusty shovel up
And loads it in the bin,
Then turns and with a healthy lunge,
That's two parts swing and two parts plunge,
He lets go at the furnace fire,
Convinced it will go in!
And then we hear a sudden smack,
The cellar air turns blue and black;

Above the rattle of the coal
We hear his awful roar.
From dreadful language upward hissed
We know that father's aim has missed,
And that his shovel full of coal
Went up against the door.

The minister was here one day
For supper, and Pa went away
To fix the furnace fire, and soon
We heard that awful roar.
And through the furnace pipes there came
Hot words that made Ma blush for shame.
" It strikes me," said the minister,
" He hit the furnace door."
Ma turned away and hung her head;
" I'm so ashamed," was all she said.
And then the minister replied:
" Don't worry. I admit
That when I hit the furnace door,
And spill the coal upon the floor,
I quite forget the cloth I wear
And — er — swear a little bit."

Out Fishin'

A feller isn't thinkin' mean,
  Out fishin';
His thoughts are mostly good an' clean,
  Out fishin'.
He doesn't knock his fellow men,
Or harbor any grudges then;
A feller's at his finest when
  Out fishin'.

The rich are comrades to the poor,
  Out fishin';
All brothers of a common lure,
  Out fishin'.
The urchin with the pin an' string
Can chum with millionaire an' king;
Vain pride is a forgotten thing,
  Out fishin'.

A feller gits a chance to dream,
  Out fishin';
He learns the beauties of a stream,
  Out fishin';
An' he can wash his soul in air
That isn't foul with selfish care,
An' relish plain and simple fare,
  Out fishin'.

A feller has no time fer hate,
    Out fishin';
He isn't eager to be great,
    Out fishin'.
He isn't thinkin' thoughts of pelf,
Or goods stacked high upon a shelf,
But he is always just himself,
    Out fishin'.

A feller's glad to be a friend,
    Out fishin';
A helpin' hand he'll always lend,
    Out fishin'.
The brotherhood of rod an' line
An' sky and stream is always fine;
Men come real close to God's design,
    Out fishin'.

A feller isn't plotting schemes,
    Out fishin';
He's only busy with his dreams,
    Out fishin'.
His livery is a coat of tan,
His creed — to do the best he can;
A feller's always mostly man,
    Out fishin'.

The little house has grown too small, or rather
    we have grown
Too big to dwell within the walls where all our
    joys were known.
And so, obedient to the wish of her we love so
    well,
I have agreed for sordid gold the little home to
    sell.
Now strangers come to see the place, and secretly
    I sigh,
And deep within my breast I hope that they'll
    refuse to buy.

"This bedroom's small," one woman said; up
    went her nose in scorn!
To me that is the splendid room where little
    Bud was born.
"The walls are sadly finger-marked," another
    stranger said.
A lump came rising in my throat; I felt my
    cheeks grow red.
"Yes, yes," I answered, "so they are. The
    fingermarks are free
But I'd not leave them here if I could take them
    all with me."

The stairway shows the signs of wear." I
    answered her in heat,
" That's but the glorious sign to me of happy
    little feet.
Most anyone can have a flight of shiny stairs
    and new
But those are steps where joy has raced, and love
    and laughter, too."
" This paper's ruined! Here are scrawled some
    pencil marks, I note."
I'd treasured them for years. They were the
    first he ever wrote.

Oh I suppose we'll sell the place; it's right that
    we should go;
The children must have larger rooms in which
    to live and grow.
But all my joys were cradled here; 'tis here I've
    lived my best,
'Tis here, whatever else shall come, we've been
    our happiest;
And though into a stranger's hands this home I
    shall resign,
And take his gold in pay for it, I still shall call
    it mine.

Daddies

I would rather be the daddy
    Of a romping, roguish crew,
Of a bright-eyed chubby laddie
    And a little girl or two,
Than the monarch of a nation,
    In his high and lofty seat,
Taking empty adoration
    From the subjects at his feet.

I would rather own their kisses,
    As at night to me they run,
Than to be the king who misses
    All the simpler forms of fun.
When his dreary day is ending
    He is dismally alone,
But when my sun is descending
    There are joys for me to own.

He may ride to horns and drumming;
    I must walk a quiet street,
But when once they see me coming,
    Then on joyous, flying feet
They come racing to me madly
    And I catch them with a swing,
And I say it proudly, gladly,
    That I'm happier than a king.

You may talk of lofty places;
    You may boast of pomp and power;
Men may turn their eager faces
    To the glory of an hour,
But give me the humble station
    With its joys that long survive,
For the daddies of the nation
    Are the happiest men alive.

Picture Books

I hold the finest picture books
Are woods an' fields an' runnin' brooks;
An' when the month o' May has done
Her paintin', an' the mornin' sun
Is lightin' just exactly right
Each gorgeous scene for mortal sight,
I steal a day from toil an' go
To see the springtime's picture show.

It's everywhere I choose to tread —
Perhaps I'll find a violet bed
Half hidden by the larger scenes,
Or group of ferns, or living greens,
So graceful an' so fine, I'll swear
That angels must have placed them there
To beautify the lonely spot
That mortal man would have forgot.

What hand can paint a picture book
So marvelous as a runnin' brook?
It matters not what time o' day
You visit it, the sunbeams play
Upon it just exactly right,
The mysteries of God to light.
No human brush could ever trace
A droopin' willow with such grace!

Page after page, new beauties rise
To thrill with gladness an' surprise
The soul of him who drops his care
And seeks the woods to wander there.
Birds, with the angel gift o' song,
Make music for him all day long;
An' nothin' that is base or mean
Disturbs the grandeur of the scene.

There is no hint of hate or strife;
The woods display the joy of life,
An' answer with a silence fine
The scoffer's jeer at power divine.
When doubt is high an' faith is low,
Back to the woods an' fields I go,
An' say to violet and tree:
" No mortal hand has fashioned thee."

Mother's Job

I'm just the man to make things right,
To mend a sleigh or make a kite,
Or wrestle on the floor and play
Those rough and tumble games, but say!
Just let him get an ache or pain,
And start to whimper and complain,
And from my side he'll quickly flee
To clamber on his mother's knee.

I'm good enough to be his horse
And race with him along the course.
I'm just the friend he wants each time
There is a tree he'd like to climb,
And I'm the pal he's eager for
When we approach a candy store;
But for his mother straight he makes
Whene'er his little stomach aches.

He likes, when he is feeling well,
The kind of stories that I tell,
And I'm his comrade and his chum
And I must march behind his drum.
To me through thick and thin he'll stick,
Unless he happens to be sick.
In which event, with me he's through —
Only his mother then will do.

The Approach of Christmas

There's a little chap at our house that is being
      mighty good —
Keeps the front lawn looking tidy in the way
      we've said he should;
Doesn't leave his little wagon, when he's finished
      with his play,
On the sidewalk as he used to; now he puts it
      right away.
When we call him in to supper, we don't have to
      stand and shout;
It is getting on to Christmas and it's plain he's
      found it out.

He eats the food we give him without murmur
      or complaint;
He sits up at the table like a cherub or a saint;
He doesn't pinch his sister just to hear how loud
      she'll squeal;
Doesn't ask us to excuse him in the middle of the
      meal,
And at eight o'clock he's willing to be tucked
      away in bed.
It is getting close to Christmas; nothing further
      need be said.

I chuckle every evening as I see that little elf,

With the crooked part proclaiming that he
    brushed his hair himself.
And I chuckle as I notice that his hands and face
    are clean,
For in him a perfect copy of another boy is
    seen —
A little boy at Christmas, who was also being
    good,
Never guessing that his father and his mother
    understood.

There's a little boy at our house that is being
    mighty good;
Doing everything that's proper, doing everything
    he should.
But besides him there's a grown-up who has
    learned life's bitter truth,
Who is gladly living over all the joys of vanished
    youth.
And although he little knows it (for it's what I
    never knew),
There's a mighty happy father sitting at the table,
    too.

The Bride

Little lady at the altar,
Vowing by God's book and psalter
To be faithful, fond and true
Unto him who stands by you,
Think not that romance is ended,
That youth's curtain has descended,
And love's pretty play is done;
For it's only just begun.

Marriage, blushing little lady,
Is love's sunny path and shady,
Over which two hearts should wander,
Of each other growing fonder.
As you stroll to each to-morrow,
You will come to joy and sorrow,
And as faithful man and wife
Read the troubled book of life.

Bitter cares will some day find you;
Closer, closer they will bind you;
If together you will bear them,
Cares grow sweet when lovers share them.
Love unites two happy mortals,
Brings them here to wedlock's portals
And then blithely bids them go,
Arm in arm, through weal and woe.

Little lady, just remember
Every year has its December,
Every rising sun its setting,
Every life its time of fretting;
And the honeymoon's sweet beauty
Finds too soon the clouds of duty;
But keep faith, when trouble-tried,
And in joy you shall abide.

Little lady at the altar,
Never let your courage falter,
Never stoop to unbelieving,
Even when your heart is grieving.
To what comes of wintry weather
Or disaster, stand together;
Through life's fearful hours of night
Love shall bring you to the light.

An Apple Tree in France

An apple tree beside the way,
Drinking the sunshine day by day
According to the Master's plan,
Had been a faithful friend to man.
It had been kind to all who came,
Nor asked the traveler's race or name,
But with the peasant boy or king
Had shared its blossoms in the spring,
And from the summer's dreary heat
To all had offered sweet retreat.

When autumn brought the harvest time,
Its branches all who wished might climb,
And take from many a tender shoot
Its rosy-cheeked, delicious fruit.
Good men, by careless speech or deed,
Have caused a neighbor's heart to bleed;
Wrong has been done by high intent;
Hate has been born where love was meant.
Yet apple trees of field or farm
Have never done one mortal harm.

Then came the Germans into France
And found this apple tree by chance.
They shared its blossoms in the spring;
They heard the songs the thrushes sing;
They rested in the cooling shade

Its old and friendly branches made,
And in the fall its fruit they ate.
And then they turn on it in hate,
Like beasts, on blood and passion drunk,
They hewed great gashes in its trunk.

Beneath its roots, with hell's delight,
They placed destruction's dynamite
And blew to death, with impish glee,
An old and friendly apple tree.
Men may rebuild their homes in time;
Swiftly cathedral towers may climb,
And hearts forget their weight of woe,
As over them life's currents flow,
But this their lasting shame shall be:
They put to death an apple tree!

Along the Paths o' Glory

Along the paths o' glory there are faces new
    to-day,
There are youthful hearts and sturdy that have
    found the westward way.
From the rugged roads o' duty they have turned
    without a sigh,
To mingle with their brothers who were not
    afraid to die.

And they're looking back and smiling at the loved
    ones left behind,
With the Old Flag flying o'er them, and they're
    calling " Never mind.
" Never mind, oh, gentle mothers, that we shall
    not come again;
Never mind the years of absence, never mind the
    days of pain,
For we've found the paths o' glory where the
    flags o' freedom fly,
And we've learned the things we died for are the
    truths that never die.
Now there's never hurt can harm us, and the
    years will never fade
The memory of the soldiers of the legions
    unafraid."

Along the paths o' glory there are faces new
    to-day,
And the heavenly flags are flying as they march
    along the way;
For the world is safe from hatred; men shall
    know it at its best
By the sacrifice and courage of the boys who go
    to rest.
Now they've claimed eternal splendor and they've
    won eternal youth,
And they've joined the gallant legions of the men
    who served the truth.

Cliffs of Scotland

Sixteen Americans who died on the Tuscania are buried at the water's edge at the base of the rocky cliffs at a Scottish port.—(News Dispatch.)

Cliffs of Scotland, guard them well,
    Shield them from the blizzard's rage;
Let your granite towers tell
That those sleeping heroes fell
    In the service of their age.

Cliffs of Scotland, they were ours!
    Now forever they are thine!
Guard them with your mighty powers!
Barren are your rocks of flowers,
    But their splendor makes them fine.

Cliffs of Scotland, at your base
    Freedom's finest children lie;
Keep them in your strong embrace!
Tell the young of every race
    Such as they shall never die.

Cliffs of Scotland, never more
    Men shall think you stern and cold;
Splendor now has found your shore;
Unto you the ocean bore
    Freedom's precious sons to hold.

Mother's Party Dress

" Some day," says Ma, " I'm goin' to get
A party dress all trimmed with jet,
An' hire a seamstress in, an' she
Is goin' to fit it right on me;
An' then, when I'm invited out
To teas an' socials hereabout,
I'll put it on an' look as fine
As all th' women friends of mine."
An' Pa looked up: " I sold a cow,"
Says he, " go down an' get it now."
An' Ma replied: " I guess I'll wait,
We've other needs that's just as great.
The children need some clothes to wear,
An' there are shoes we must repair;
It ain't important now to get
A dress fer me, at least not yet;
 I really can't afford it."

Ma's talked about that dress fer years;
How she'd have appliqued revers;
The kind o' trimmin' she would pick;
How 't would be made to fit her slick;
The kind o' black silk she would choose,
The pattern she would like to use.
An' I can mind the time when Pa
Give twenty dollars right to Ma,
An' said: " Now that's enough, I guess,

Go buy yourself that party dress."
An' Ma would take th' bills an' smile,
An' say: " I guess I'll wait awhile;
Aunt Kitty's poorly now with chills
She needs a doctor and some pills;
I'll buy some things fer her, I guess;
An' anyhow, about that dress,
      I really can't afford it."

An' so it's been a-goin' on,
Her dress fer other things has gone;
Some one in need or some one sick
Has always touched her to th' quick;
Or else, about th' time 'at she
Could get th' dress, she'd always see
The children needin' somethin' new;
An' she would go an' get it, too.
An' when we frowned at her, she'd smile
An' say: " The dress can wait awhile."
Although her mind is set on laces,
Her heart goes out to other places;
An' somehow, too, her money goes
In ways that only mother knows.
While there are things her children lack
She won't put money on her back;
An' that is why she hasn't got
A party dress of silk, an' not
      Because she can't afford it.

Little Fishermen

A little ship goes out to sea
As soon as we have finished tea;
Off yonder where the big moon glows
This tiny little vessel goes,
But never grown-up eyes have seen
The ports to which this ship has been;
Upon the shore the old folks stand
Till morning brings it back to land.

In search of smiles this little ship
Each evening starts upon a trip;
Just smiles enough to last the day
Is it allowed to bring away;
So nightly to some golden shore
It must set out alone for more,
And sail the rippling sea for miles
Until the hold is full of smiles.

By gentle hands the sails are spread;
The stars are glistening overhead
And in that hour when tiny ships
Prepare to make their evening trips
The sea becomes a wondrous place,
As beautiful as mother's face;
And all the day's disturbing cries
Give way to soothing lullabies.

No clang of bell or warning shout
Is heard on shore when they put out;
The little vessels slip away
As silently as does the day.
And all night long on sands of gold
They cast their nets, and fill the hold
With smiles and joys beyond compare,
To cheer a world that's sad with care.

The Cookie-Lady

She is gentle, kind and fair,
And there's silver in her hair;
She has known the touch of sorrow,
But the smile of her is sweet;
And sometimes it seems to me
That her mission is to be
The gracious cookie-lady
To the youngsters of the street.

All the children in the block
Daily stand beside the crock,
Where she keeps the sugar cookies
That the little folks enjoy;
And no morning passes o'er
That a tapping at her door
Doesn't warn her of the visit
Of a certain little boy.

She has made him feel that he
Has a natural right to be
In her kitchen when she's baking
Pies and cakes and ginger bread;
And each night to me he brings
All the pretty, tender things
About little by-gone children
That the cookie-lady said.

Oh, dear cookie-lady sweet,
May you beautify our street
With your kind and gentle presence
Many more glad years, I pray;
May the skies be bright above you,
As you've taught our babes to love you;
You will scar their hearts with sorrow
If you ever go away.

Life is strange, and when I scan it,
I believe God tries to plan it,
So that where He sends his babies
In that neighborhood to dwell,
One of rare and gracious beauty
Shall abide, whose sweetest duty
Is to be the cookie-lady
That the children love so well.

Pleasure's Signs

There's a bump on his brow and a smear on his
      cheek
    That is plainly the stain of his tears;
At his neck there's a glorious sun-painted streak,
    The bronze of his happiest years.
Oh, he's battered and bruised at the end of the
      day,
    But smiling before me he stands,
And somehow I like to behold him that way.
    Yes, I like him with dirt on his hands.

Last evening he painfully limped up to me
    His tale of adventure to tell;
He showed me a grime-covered cut on his knee,
    And told me the place where he fell.
His clothing was stained to the color of clay,
    And he looked to be nobody's lad,
But somehow I liked to behold him that way,
    For it spoke of the fun that he'd had.

Let women-folk prate as they will of a boy
    Who is heedless of knickers and shirt;
I hold that the badge of a young fellow's joy
    Are cheeks that are covered with dirt.
So I look for him nightly to greet me that way,
    His joys and misfortunes to tell,
For I know by the signs that he wears of his
      play
    That the lad I'm so fond of is well.

Snooping 'Round

Last night I caught him on his knees and looking
    underneath the bed,
And oh, the guilty look he wore, and oh, the
    stammered words he said,
When I, pretending to be cross, said: "Hey,
    young fellow, what's your game?"
As if, back in the long ago, I hadn't also played
    the same;
As if, upon my hands and knees, I hadn't many
    a time been found
When, thinking of the Christmas Day, I'd gone
    upstairs to snoop around.

But there he stood and hung his head; the rascal
    knew it wasn't fair.
"I jes' was wonderin'," he said, "jes' what it
    was that's under there.
It's somepin' all wrapped up an' I thought mebbe
    it might be a sled,
Becoz I saw a piece of wood 'at's stickin' out
    all painted red."
"If mother knew," I said to him, "you'd get a
    licking, I'll be bound,
But just clear out of here at once, and don't you
    ever snoop around."

And as he scampered down the stairs I stood and
    chuckled to myself,

As I remembered how I'd oft explored the top-
   most closet shelf.
It all came back again to me — with what a
   shrewd and cunning way
I, too, had often sought to solve the mysteries of
   Christmas Day.
How many times my daddy, too, had come up-
   stairs without a sound
And caught me, just as I'd begun my clever
   scheme to snoop around.

And oh, I envied him his plight; I envied him
   the joy he feels
Who knows that every drawer that's locked some
   treasure dear to him conceals;
I envied him his Christmas fun and wished that
   it again were mine
To seek to solve the mysteries by paper wrapped
   and bound by twine.
Some day he'll come to understand that all the
   time I stood and frowned,
I saw a boy of years ago who also used to snoop
   around.

Bud Discusses Cleanliness

First thing in the morning, last I hear at night
Get it when I come from school: " My, you look
    a sight!
Go upstairs this minute, an' roll your sleeves
    up high
An' give your hands a scrubbing and wipe 'em
    till they're dry!
Now don't stand there and argue, and never
    mind your tears!
And this time please remember to wash your
    neck and ears."

Can't see why ears grow on us, all crinkled like
    a shell,
With lots of fancy carvings that make a feller
    yell
Each time his Ma digs in them to get a speck
    of dirt,
When plain ones would be easy to wash and
    wouldn't hurt.
And I can't see the reason why every time Ma
    nears,
She thinks she's got to send me to wash my
    neck and ears.

I never wash to suit her; don't think I ever will.
If I was white as sister, she'd call me dirty still.

At night I get a scrubbing and go to bed, and
      then
The first thing in the morning, she makes me
      wash again.
That strikes me as ridiklus; I've thought of
      it a heap.
A feller can't get dirty when he is fast asleep.

When I grow up to be a man like Pa, and
      have a wife
And kids to boss around, you bet they'll have
      an easy life.
We won't be at them all the time, the way they
      keep at me,
And kick about a little dirt that no one else
      can see.
And every night at supper time as soon as he
      appears,
We will not chase our boy away to wash his
      neck and ears.

Tied Down

" They tie you down," a woman said,
Whose cheeks should have been flaming red
With shame to speak of children so.
" When babies come you cannot go
In search of pleasure with your friends,
And all your happy wandering ends.
The things you like you cannot do,
For babies make a slave of you."

I looked at her and said: " 'Tis true
That children make a slave of you,
And tie you down with many a knot,
But have you never thought to what
It is of happiness and pride
That little babies have you tied?
Do you not miss the greater joys
That come with little girls and boys?

" They tie you down to laughter rare,
To hours of smiles and hours of care,
To nights of watching and to fears;
Sometimes they tie you down to tears
And then repay you with a smile,
And make your trouble all worth while.
They tie you fast to chubby feet,
And cheeks of pink and kisses sweet.

" They fasten you with cords of love
To God divine, who reigns above.
They tie you, whereso'er you roam,
Unto the little place called home;
And over sea or railroad track
They tug at you to bring you back.
The happiest people in the town
Are those the babies have tied down.

" Oh, go your selfish way and free,
But hampered I would rather be,
Yes rather than a kingly crown
I would be, what you term, tied down;
Tied down to dancing eyes and charms,
Held fast by chubby, dimpled arms,
The fettered slave of girl and boy,
And win from them earth's finest joy."

Our Country

God grant that we shall never see
   Our country slave to lust and greed;
God grant that here all men shall be
   United by a common creed.
Here Freedom's Flag has held the sky
   Unstained, untarnished from its birth;
Long may it wave to typify
   The happiest people on the earth.

Beneath its folds have mothers smiled
   To see their little ones at play;
No tyrant hand, by shame defiled,
   To them has barred life's rosy way.
No cruel wall of caste or class
   Has bid men pause or turn aside;
Here looms no gate they may not pass —
   Here every door is opened wide.

Here at the wells of Freedom all
   Who are athirst may drink their fill.
Here fame and fortune wait to call
   The toiler who has proved his skill.
Here wisdom sheds afar its light
   As every morn the school bells ring,
And little children read and write
   And share the knowledge of a king.

God grant that we shall never see
    Our country slave to lust and greed;
God grant that men shall always be
    United for our nation's need.
Here selfishness has never reigned,
    Here freedom all who come may know;
By tyranny our Flag's unstained!
    God grant that we may keep it so.

Fatherhood

Before you came, my little lad,
    I used to think that I was good;
Some vicious habits, too, I had,
    But wouldn't change them if I could.
I held my head up high and said:
    "I'm all that I have need to be,
It matters not what path I tread —
    But that was ere you came to me.

I treated lightly sacred things,
    And went my way in search of fun;
Upon myself I kept no strings,
    And gave no heed to folly done.
I gave myself up to the fight
    For worldly wealth and earthly fame,
And sought advantage, wrong or right —
    But that was long before you came.

77

But now you sit across from me,
     Your big brown eyes are opened wide,
And every deed I do you see,
     And, O, I dare not step aside.
I've shaken loose from habits bad,
     And what is wrong I've come to dread,
Because I know, my little lad,
     That you will follow where I tread.

I want those eyes to glow with pride;
     In me, I want those eyes to see,
The while we wander side by side,
     The sort of man I'd have you be.
And so I'm striving to be good
     With all my might, that you may know,
When this great world is understood,
     What pleasures are worth while below.

I see life in a different light
     From what I did before you came;
Then anything that pleased seemed right —
     But you are here to bear my name,
And you are looking up to me
     With those big eyes from day to day,
And I'm determined not to be —
     The means of leading you astray.

A Choice

Sure, they get stubborn at times; they worry and
      fret us a lot,
But I'd rather be crossed by a glad little boy and
      frequently worried than not.
There are hours when they get on my nerves
      and set my poor brain all awhirl,
But I'd rather be troubled that way than to be
      the man who has no little girl.

There are times they're a nuisance, that's true,
      with all of their racket and noise,
But I'd rather my personal pleasures be lost than
      to give up my girls and my boys.
Not always they're perfectly good; there are
      times when they're wilfully bad,
But I'd rather be worried by youngsters of mine
      than lonely and childless and sad.

So I try to be patient and calm whenever they're
      having their fling;
For the sum of their laughter and love is more
      than the worry they bring.
And each night when sweet peace settles down
      and I see them asleep in their cot,
I chuckle and say: "They upset me to-day, but
      I'd rather be that way than not."

What Father Knows

My father knows the proper way
    The nation should be run;
He tells us children every day
    Just what should now be done.
He knows the way to fix the trusts,
    He has a simple plan;
But if the furnace needs repairs
    We have to hire a man.

My father, in a day or two,
    Could land big thieves in jail;
There's nothing that he cannot do,
    He knows no word like " fail."
" Our confidence " he would restore,
    Of that there is no doubt;
But if there is a chair to mend
    We have to send it out.

All public questions that arise
    He settles on the spot;
He waits not till the tumult dies,
    But grabs it while it's hot.
In matters of finance he can
    Tell Congress what to do;
But, O, he finds it hard to meet
    His bills as they fall due.

It almost makes him sick to read
    The things law-makers say;
Why, father's just the man they need;
    He never goes astray.
All wars he'd very quickly end,
    As fast as I can write it;
But when a neighbor starts a fuss
    'Tis mother has to fight it.

In conversation father can
    Do many wondrous things;
He's built upon a wiser plan
    Than presidents or kings.
He knows the ins and outs of each
    And every deep transaction;
We look to him for theories,
    But look to ma for action.

Back Home

Glad to get back home again,
Where abide the friendly men;
Glad to see the same old scenes
And the little house that means
All the joys the soul has treasured —
Glad to be where smiles aren't measured,
Where I've blended with the gladness
All the heart has known of sadness,
Where some long-familiar steeple
Marks my town of friendly people.

Though it's fun to go a-straying
Where the bands are nightly playing
And the throngs of men and women
Drain the cup of pleasure brimmin',
I am glad when it is over
That I've ceased to play the Rover.
And when once the train starts chugging
Towards the children I'd be hugging,
All my thoughts and dreams are set there;
Fast enough I cannot get there.

Guess I wasn't meant for bright lights,
For the blaze of red and white lights,
For the throngs that seems to smother
In their selfishness, each other;
For whenever I've been down there,

Tramped the noisy, blatant town there,
Always in a week I've started
Yearning, hungering, heavy-hearted,
For the home town and its spaces
Lit by fine and friendly faces.

Like to be where men about me
Do not look on me to doubt me;
Where I know the men and women,
Know why tears some eyes are dimmin',
Know the good folks an' the bad folks
An' the glad folks an' the sad folks;
Where we live with one another,
Meanin' something to each other.
An' I'm glad to see the steeple,
Where the crowds aren't merely people.

The Dead Return

The dead return. I know they do;
The glad smile may have passed from view,
The ringing voice that cheered us so
In that remembered long ago
Be stilled, and yet in sweeter ways
It speaks to us throughout our days.
The kindly father comes again
To guide us through the haunts of men,
And always near, their sons to greet
Are lingering the mothers sweet.

About us wheresoe'er we tread
Hover the spirits of our dead;
We cannot see them as we could
In bygone days, when near they stood
And shared the joys and griefs that came,
But they are with us just the same.
They see us as we plod along,
And proudly smile when we are strong,
And sigh and grieve the self-same way
When thoughtlessly we go astray.

I sometimes think it hurts the dead
When into sin and shame we're led,
And that they feel a thrill divine
When we've accomplished something fine.
And sometimes thoughts that come at night

Seem more like messages that might
Have whispered been by one we love,
Whose spirit has been called above.
So wise the counsel, it must be
That all we are the dead can see.

The dead return. They come to share
Our laughter and our bit of care;
They glory, as they used to do,
When we are splendid men and true,
In all the joy that we have won,
And they are proud of what we've done.
They suffer when we suffer woe;
All things about us here they know.
And though we never see them here
Their spirits hover very near.

My Soul and I

When winter shuts a fellow in and turns the
    lock upon his door,
There's nothing else for him to do but sit and
    dream his bygones o'er.
And then before an open fire he smokes his pipe
    while in the blaze
He seems to see a picture show of all his happy
    yesterdays.
No ordinary film is that which memory throws
    upon the screen,
But one in which his hidden soul comes out and
    can be plainly seen.

Now, I've been dreaming by the grate. I've seen
    myself the way I am,
Stripped bare of affectation's garb and wisdom's
    pose and folly's sham.
I've seen my soul and talked with it, and learned
    some things I never knew.
I walk about the world as one, but I express the
    wish of two.
I've come to see the soul of me is wiser than my
    selfish mind,
For it has safely led me through the tangled
    paths I've left behind.

I should have sold myself for gold when I was
  young long years ago,
But for my soul which whispered then: " You
  love your home and garden so,
You never could be quite content in palace walls.
  Once rise to fame
And you will lose the gentler joys which now so
  eagerly you claim.
I want to walk these lanes with you and keep the
  comradeship of trees,
Let you and I be happy here, nor seek life's
  gaudy luxuries."

Mine is a curious soul, I guess; it seemed so,
  smiling in my dreams;
It keeps me close to little folks and birds and
  flowers and running streams,
To Mother and her friends and mine; and though
  no fortune we possess,
The years that we have lived and loved have all
  been rich with happiness.
I'm glad the snowdrifts shut me in, for I have
  had a chance to see
How fortunate I've been to have that sort of
  soul to counsel me.

Aunty

I'm sorry for a feller if he hasn't any aunt,
To let him eat and do the things his mother says
    he can't.
An aunt to come a visitin' or one to go and see
Is just about the finest kind of lady there could be.
Of course she's not your mother, an' she hasn't
    got her ways,
But a part that's most important in a feller's life
    she plays.

She is kind an' she is gentle, an' sometimes she's
    full of fun,
An' she's very sympathetic when some dreadful
    thing you've done.
An' she likes to buy you candy, an' she's always
    gettin' toys
That you wish your Pa would get you, for she
    hasn't any boys.
But sometimes she's over-loving, an' your cheeks
    turn red with shame
When she smothers you with kisses, but you like
    her just the same.

One time my father took me to my aunty's, an'
    he said:
" You will stay here till I get you, an' be sure you
    go to bed

When your aunty says it's time to, an' be good
  an' mind her, too,
An' when you come home we'll try to have a big
  surprise for you."
I did as I was told to, an' when Pa came back
  for me
He said there was a baby at the house for me
  to see.

I've been visitin' at aunty's for a week or two,
  an' Pa
Has written that he's comin' soon to take me
  home to Ma.
He says they're gettin' lonely, an' I'm kind o'
  lonely, too,
Coz an aunt is not exactly what your mother is
  to you.
I am hungry now to see her, but I'm wondering
  to-day
If Pa's bought another baby in the time I've been
  away.

Bread and Jam

I wish I was a poet like the men that write in
    books
The poems that we have to learn on valleys,
    hills an' brooks;
I'd write of things that children like an' know
    an' understand,
An' when the kids recited them the folks would
    call them grand.
If I'd been born a Whittier, instead of what I
    am,
I'd write a poem now about a piece of bread
    an' jam.

I'd tell how hungry children get all afternoon in
    school,
An' sittin' at attention just because it is the rule,
An' lookin' every now an' then up to the clock
    to see
If that big hand an' little hand would ever get
    to three.
I'd tell how children hurry home an' give the
    door a slam
An' ask their mothers can they have a piece of
    bread an' jam.

Some poets write of things to eat an' sing of
    dinners fine,

An' praise the dishes they enjoy, an' some folks
      sing of wine,
But they've forgotten, I suppose, the days when
      they were small
An' hurried home from school to get the finest
      food of all;
They don't remember any more how good it
      was to cram
Inside their hungry little selves a piece of bread
      an' jam.

I wish I was a Whittier, a Stevenson or Burns,
I wouldn't write of hills an' brooks, or mossy
      banks or ferns,
I wouldn't write of rolling seas or mountains
      towering high,
But I would sing of chocolate cake an' good old
      apple pie,
An' best of all the food there is, beyond the
      slightest doubt,
Is bread an' jam we always get as soon as school
      is out.

The Little Woman

The little woman, to her I bow
   And doff my hat as I pass her by;
I reverence the furrows that mark her brow,
   And the sparkling love light in her eye.
The little woman who stays at home,
   And makes no bid for the world's applause;
Who never sighs for a chance to roam,
   But toils all day in a grander cause.

The little woman, who seems so weak,
   Yet bears her burdens day by day;
And no one has ever heard her speak
   In a bitter or loud complaining way.
She sings a snatch of a merry song,
   As she toils in her home from morn to night.
Her work is hard and the hours are long
   But the little woman's heart is light.

A slave to love is that woman small,
   And yearly her burdens heavier grow,
But somehow she seems to bear them all,
   As the deep'ning lines in her white cheeks show.
Her children all have a mother's care,
   Her home the touch of a good wife knows;
No burden's too heavy for her to bear,
   But, patiently doing her best, she goes.

The little woman, may God be kind
　　To her wherever she dwells to-day;
The little woman who seems to find
　　Her joy in toiling along life's way.
May God bring peace to her work-worn breast
　　And joy to her mother-heart at last;
May love be hers when it's time to rest,
　　And the roughest part of the road is passed.

The little woman — how oft it seems
　　God chooses her for the mother's part;
And many a grown-up sits and dreams
　　To-day of her with an aching heart.
For he knows well how she toiled for him
　　And he sees it now that it is too late;
And often his eyes with tears grow dim
　　For the little woman whose strength was great.

The Father of the Man

I can't help thinkin' o' the lad!
  Here's summer bringin' trees to fruit,
An' every bush with roses clad,
  An' nature in her finest suit,
An' all things as they used to be
  In days before the war came on.
Yet time has changed both him an' me,
  An' I am here, but he is gone.

The orchard's as it was back then
  When he was just a little tyke;
The lake's as calm an' fair as when
  We used to go to fish for pike.
There's nothing different I can see
  That God has made about the place,
Except the change in him an' me,
  An' that is difficult to trace.

I only know one day he came
  An' found me in the barn alone.
To some he might have looked the same,
  But he was not the lad I'd known.
His soul, it seemed, had heard the call
  As plainly as a mortal can.
Before he spoke to me at all,
  I saw my boy become a man.

I can't explain just what occurred;
　　I sat an' talked about it there;
The dinner-bell I never heard,
　　Or if I did, I didn't care.
But suddenly it seemed to me
　　Out of the dark there came a light,
An' in a new way I could see
　　That I was wrong an' he was right.

I can't help thinkin' o' the lad!
　　He's fightin' hate an' greed an' lust,
An' here am I, his doting dad,
　　Believin' in a purpose just.
Time was I talked the joy o' play,
　　But now life's goal is all I see;
The petty thoughts I've put away —
　　My boy has made a man o' me.

When Mother Made An Angel Cake

When mother baked an angel cake we kids would
    gather round
An' watch her gentle hands at work, an' never
    make a sound;
We'd watch her stir the eggs an' flour an' pow-
    dered sugar, too,
An' pour it in the crinkled tin, an' then when it
    was through
She'd spread the icing over it, an' we knew very
    soon
That one would get the plate to lick, an' one
    would get the spoon.

It seemed no matter where we were those morn-
    ings at our play,
Upstairs or out of doors somewhere, we all knew
    right away
When Ma was in the kitchen, an' was gettin' out
    the tin
An' things to make an angel cake, an' so we
    scampered in.
An' Ma would smile at us an' say: "Now you
    keep still an' wait
An' when I'm through I'll let you lick the spoon
    an' icing plate."

We watched her kneel beside the stove, an' put
    her arm so white
Inside the oven just to find if it was heatin' right.
An' mouths an' eyes were open then, becoz we
    always knew
The time for us to get our taste was quickly
    comin' due.
Then while she mixed the icing up, she'd hum a
    simple tune,
An' one of us would bar the plate, an' one would
    bar the spoon.

Could we catch a glimpse of Heaven, and some
    snow-white kitchen there,
I'm sure that we'd see mother, smiling now, and
    still as fair;
And I know that gathered round her we should
    see an angel brood
That is watching every movement as she makes
    an angel food;
For I know that little angels, as we used to do,
    await
The moment when she lets them lick the icing
    spoon and plate.

The Gift of Play

Some have the gift of song and some possess the
gift of silver speech,
Some have the gift of leadership and some the
ways of life can teach.
And fame and wealth reward their friends; in
jewels are their splendors told,
But in good time their favorites grow very faint
and gray and old.
But there are men who laugh at time and hold the
cruel years at bay;
They romp through life forever young because
they have the gift of play.

They walk with children, hand in hand, through
daisy fields and orchards fair,
Nor all the dignity of age and power and pomp
can follow there;
They've kept the magic charm of youth beneath
the wrinkled robe of Time,
And there's no friendly apple tree that they have
grown too old to climb.
They have not let their boyhood die; they can
be children for the day;
They have not bartered for success and all its
praise, the gift of play.

They think and talk in terms of youth; with
     love of life their eyes are bright;
No rheumatism of the soul has robbed them of
     the world's delight;
They laugh and sing their way along and join
     in pleasures when they can,
And in their glad philosophy they hold that
     mirth becomes a man.
They spend no strength in growing old. What
     if their brows be crowned with gray?
The spirits in their breasts are young. They
     still possess the gift of play.

The richest men of life are not the ones who rise
     to wealth and fame —
Not the great sages, old and wise, and grave
     of face and bent of frame,
But the glad spirits, tall and straight, who 'spite
     of time and all its care,
Have kept the power to laugh and sing and in
     youth's fellowship to share.
They that can walk with boys and be a boy
     among them, blithe and gay,
Defy the withering blasts of Age because they
     have the gift of play.

Toys and Life

You can learn a lot from boys
By the way they use their toys;
Some are selfish in their care,
Never very glad to share
Playthings with another boy;
Seem to want to hoard their joy.
And they hide away the drum
For the days that never come;
Hide the train of cars and skates,
Keeping them from all their mates,
And run all their boyhood through
With their toys as good as new.

Others gladly give and lend,
Heedless that the tin may bend,
Caring not that drum-heads break,
Minding not that playmates take
To themselves the joy that lies
In the little birthday prize.
And in homes that house such boys
Always there are broken toys,
Symbolizing moments glad
That the youthful lives have had.
There you'll never find a shelf
Dedicated unto self.

Toys are made for children's fun,

Very frail and quickly done,
And who keeps them long to view,
Bright of paint and good as new,
Robs himself and other boys
Of their swiftly passing joys.
So he looked upon a toy
When our soldier was a boy;
And somehow to-day we're glad
That the tokens of our lad
And the trinkets that we keep
Are a broken, battered heap.

Life itself is but a toy
Filled with duty and with joy;
Not too closely should we guard
Our brief time from being scarred;
Never high on musty shelves
Should we hoard it for ourselves.
It is something we should share
In another's hour of care —
Something we should gladly give
That another here may live;
We should never live it through
Keeping it as good as new.

Being Dad on Christmas Eve

They've hung their stockings up with care,
And I am in my old arm chair,
And mother's busy dragging out
The parcels hidden all about.
Within a corner, gaunt to see,
There stands a barren Christmas tree,
But soon upon its branches green
A burst of splendor will be seen.
And when the busy tongues grow still,
That now are wagging with a will
Above me as I sit and rest,
I shall be at my happiest.
The greatest joy man can receive
Is being Dad on Christmas eve.

Soon I shall toil with tinsel bright;
Place here and there a colored light,
And wheresoe'er my fingers lie
To-morrow shall a youngster spy
Some wonder gift or magic toy,
To fill his little soul with joy.
The stockings on the mantle piece
I'll bulge with sweets, till every crease
That marks them now is stretched away.
There will be horns and drums to play
And dolls to love. For it's my task
To get for them the joys they ask.

What greater charm can fortune weave
Than being Dad on Christmas eve?

With all their pomp, great monarchs miss
The happiness of scenes like this.
Rich halls to-night are still and sad,
Because no little girl or lad
Shall wake upon the morn to find
The joys that love has left behind.
Oh, I have had my share of woe —
Known what it is to bear a blow —
Shed sorrow's tears and stood to care
When life seemed desolate and bare,
Yet here to-night I smile and say
Worth while was all that came my way.
For this one joy, all else I'd leave:
To be their Dad on Christmas eve.

Little Girls

God made the little boys for fun, for rough and
       tumble times of play;
He made their little legs to run and race and
       scamper through the day.
He made them strong for climbing trees, he
       suited them for horns and drums,
And filled them full of revelries so they could be
       their father's chums.

But then He saw that gentle ways must also
    travel from above.
And so, through all our troubled days He sent
    us little girls to love.

He knew that earth would never do, unless a bit
    of Heaven it had.
Men needed eyes divinely blue to toil by day and
    still be glad.
A world where only men and boys made merry
    would in time grow stale,
And so He shared His Heavenly joys that faith
    in Him should never fail.
He sent us down a thousand charms, He decked
    our ways with golden curls
And laughing eyes and dimpled arms. He let us
    have His little girls.

They are the tenderest of His flowers, the little
    angels of His flock,
And we may keep and call them ours, until God's
    messenger shall knock.
They bring to us the gentleness and beauty that
    we sorely need;
They soothe us with each fond caress and
    strengthen us for every deed.
And happy should that mortal be whom God has
    trusted, through the years,
To guard a little girl and see that she is kept
    from pain and tears.

United States

He shall be great who serves his country well.
  He shall be loved who ever guards her fame.
His worth the starry banner long shall tell,
  Who loves his land too much to stoop to shame.

Who shares the splendor of these sunny skies
  Has freedom as his birthright, and may know
Rich fellowship with comrades brave and wise;
  Into the realms of manhood he may go.

Who writes, " United States " beside his name
  Offers a pledge that he himself is true;
Gives guarantee that selfishness or shame
  Shall never mar the work he finds to do.

He is received world-wide as one who lives
  Above the sordid dreams of petty gain,
And is reputed as a man who gives
  His best to others in their hours of pain.

This is the heritage of Freedom's soil:
  High purposes and lofty goals to claim.
And he shall be rewarded for his toil
  Who loves his land too much to stoop to
    shame.

When My Ship Comes In

You shall have satin and silk to wear,
  When my ship comes in;
And jewels to shine in your raven hair,
  When my ship comes in.
Oh, the path is dreary to-day and long,
And little I've brought to your life of song,
But the dream still lives and the faith
    is strong,
  When my ship comes in.

Gold and silver are pledged to you,
  When my ship comes in;
I pay with this promise for all you do,
  When my ship comes in.
Oh, fairest partner man ever had,
It's little I've brought you to make you glad
Save the whispered suggestion in moments
    sad,
  When my ship comes in.

Though crowded with treasures should
    be her hold,
  When my ship comes in,
I never can pay for the charms of old,
  When my ship comes in.
The strength I have taken from you has fled,
The time for the joys that you craved has
    sped,

I must pay for your gold with the dullest
   lead,
   When my ship comes in.

Too late, too late will the treasures be,
   When my ship comes in.
For Age shall stand with us on the quay,
   When my ship comes in.
For the love you've given and the faith
      you've shown,
But a glimpse of the joys that you might
      have known
Will it then be yours on that day to own,
   When my ship comes in.

The Children

The children bring us laughter, and the children
    bring us tears;
They string our joys, like jewels bright, upon
    the thread of years;
They bring the bitterest cares we know, their
    mothers' sharpest pain,
Then smile our world to loveliness, like sunshine
    after rain.

The children make us what we are; the childless
    king is spurned;
The children send us to the hills where glories
    may be earned;
For them we pledge our lives to strife, for them
    do mothers fade,
And count in new-born loveliness their sacrifice
    repaid.

The children bring us back to God; in eyes that
    dance and shine
Men read from day to day the proof of love and
    power divine;
For them are fathers brave and good and
    mothers fair and true,
For them is every cherished dream and every
    deed we do.

For children are the furnace fires of life kept
 blazing high;
For children on the battle fields are soldiers
 pleased to die;
In every place where humans toil, in every dream
 and plan,
The laughter of the children shapes the destiny
 of man.

The Comedian

Whatever the task and whatever the risk, wher-
 ever the flag's in air,
The funny man with his sunny ways is sure to
 be laughing there.
There are men who fret, there are men who
 dream, men making the best of it,
 But whether it's hunger or death they face,
 Or burning thirst in a desert place,
 There is always one, by the good Lord's grace,
Who is making a jest of it.

He travels wherever his brothers go and he leaves
 his home behind him,
The need for smiles he seems to know; in the
 ranks of death you'll find him.
When some are weary and sick and faint, and
 all with the dust are choking,

He dances there with a spirit gay,
And tints with gold what is drab and gray,
And into the gloom of the night and day
He scatters his mirthful joking.

He wins to courage the soul-tried men; he lightens
their hours of sorrow;
He turns their thoughts from the grief that is to
the joy that may come to-morrow.
He mocks at death and he jests at toil, as one
that is never weary;
He japes at danger and discipline,
Or the muddy trench that he's standing in;
There's nothing can banish his merry grin,
Or dampen his spirits cheery.

The honors of war to its heroes go; for them are
the pomp and glory,
But seldom it is that the types relate a victory's
inside story.
And few shall know when the strife is done and
the history's made hereafter,
How much depended on him who stirred
The souls of men with a cheerful word,
And kept them brave by a jest absurd,
And brightened their days with laughter.

Faith

It is faith that bridges the land of breath
    To the realms of the souls departed,
That comforts the living in days of death,
    And strengthens the heavy-hearted.
It is faith in his dreams that keeps a man
    Face front to the odds about him,
And he shall conquer who thinks he can,
    In spite of the throngs who doubt him.

Each must stand in the court of life
    And pass through the hours of trial;
He shall tested be by the rules of strife,
    And tried for his self-denial.
Time shall bruise his soul with the loss of friends,
    And frighten him with disaster,
But he shall find when the anguish ends
    That of all things faith is master.

So keep your faith in the God above,
    And faith in the righteous truth,
It shall bring you back to the absent love,
    And the joys of a vanished youth.
You shall smile once more when your tears are
      dried,
    Meet trouble and swiftly rout it,
For faith is the strength of the soul inside,
    And lost is the man without it.

The Burden Bearer

Oh, my shoulders grow aweary of the burdens
    I am bearin',
An' I grumble when I'm footsore at the rough
    road I am farin',
But I strap my knapsack tighter till I feel the
    leather bind me,
An' I'm glad to bear the burdens for the ones
    who come behind me.
It's for them that I am ploddin', for the chil-
    dren comin' after;
I would strew their path with roses and would
    fill their days with laughter.

Oh, there's selfishness within me, there are times
    it gets to talkin',
Times I hear it whisper to me, "It's a dusty
    road you're walkin';
Why not rest your feet a little; why not pause an'
    take your leisure?
Don't you hunger in your strivin' for the merry
    whirl of pleasure?"
Then I turn an' see them smilin' an' I grip my
    burdens tighter,
For the joy that I am seekin' is to see their eyes
    grow brighter.

Oh, I've sipped the cup of sorrow an' I've felt
  the gad of trouble,
An' I know the hurt of trudgin' through a field
  o'errun with stubble;
But a rougher road to travel had my father good
  before me,
An' I'm owin' all my gladness to the tasks he
  shouldered for me.
Oh, I didn't understand it, when a lad I played
  about him,
But he labored for my safety in the days I'd
  be without him.

Oh, my kindly father never gave himself a year
  of leisure —
Never lived one selfish moment, never turned
  aside for pleasure —
Though he must have grown aweary of the burdens he was bearin';
He was tryin' hard to better every road I'd
  soon be farin'.
Now I turn an' see them smilin' an' I hear their
  merry laughter,
An' I'm glad to bear the burdens for the ones
  that follow after.

"It's a Boy"

The doctor leads a busy life, he wages war with
    death;
Long hours he spends to help the one who's fight-
    ing hard for breath;
He cannot call his time his own, nor share in
    others' fun,
His duties claim him through the night when
    others' work is done.
And yet the doctor seems to be God's messenger
    of joy,
Appointed to announce this news of gladness:
    "It's a boy!"

In many ways unpleasant is the doctor's round
    of cares,
I should not like to have to bear the burdens
    that he bears;
His eyes must look on horrors grim, unmoved
    he must remain,
Emotion he must master if he hopes to conquer
    pain;
Yet to his lot this duty falls, his voice he must
    employ
To speak to man the happiest phrase that's
    sounded: "It's a boy!"

I wish 'twere given me to speak a message half
    so glad

As that the doctor brings unto the fear-distracted
      dad.
I wish that simple words of mine could change
      the skies to blue,
And lift the care from troubled hearts, as those
      he utters do.
I wish that I could banish all the thoughts that
      man annoy,
And cheer him as the doctor does, who whispers:
      " It's a boy."

Whoever through the hours of night has stood
      outside her door,
And wondered if she'd smile again; whoe'er has
      paced the floor,
And lived those years of fearful thoughts, and
      then been swept from woe
Up to the topmost height of bliss that's given
      man to know,
Will tell you there's no phrase so sweet, so
      charged with human joy
As that the doctor brings from God — that mes-
      sage: " It's a boy! "

The Finest Fellowship

There may be finer pleasures than just tramping
. with your boy,
And better ways to spend a day; there may be
sweeter joy;
There may be richer fellowship than that of son
and dad,
But if there is, I know it not; it's one I've never
had.

Oh, some may choose to walk with kings and
men of pomp and pride,
But as for me, I choose to have my youngster at
my side.
And some may like the rosy ways of grown-up
pleasures glad,
But I would go a-wandering with just a little
lad.

Yes, I would seek the woods with him and talk
to him of trees,
And learn to know the birds a-wing and hear
their melodies;
And I would drop all worldly care and be a boy
awhile;
Then hand-in-hand come home at dusk to see
the mother smile.

Grown men are wearisome at times, and selfish
        pleasures jar,
But sons and dads throughout the world the
        truest comrades are.
So when I want a perfect day with every joy
        that's fine,
I spend it in the open with that little lad o' mine.

Different

The kids at our house number three,
As different as they can be;
And if perchance they numbered six
Each one would have particular tricks,
And certain little whims and fads
Unlike the other girls and lads.
No two glad rascals can you name
Whom God has fashioned just the same.

Bud's tough and full of life and fun
And likes to race about and run,
And tease the girls; the rascal knows
The slyest ways to pinch a nose,
And yank a curl until it hurts,
And disarrange their Sunday skirts.
Sometimes he trips them, heads o'er heels,
To glory in their frenzied squeals.

And Marjorie: She'd have more joy,
She thinks, if she'd been born a boy;
She wants no ribbons on her hair,
No fancy, fussy things to wear.
The things in which Sylvia delights
To Marjorie are dreadful frights.
They're sisters, yet I'd swear the name
Is all they own that is the same.

Proud Sylvia, beautiful to see,
A high-toned lady wants to be;
She'll primp and fuss and deck her hair
And gorgeous raiment wants to wear;
She'll sit sedately by the light
And read a fairy tale at night;
And she will sigh and sometimes wince
At all the trials of the prince.

If God should send us children nine
To follow our ancestral line,
I'd vow that in the lot we'd strike
No two among them just alike.
And that's the way it ought to be;
The larger grows the family,
The more we own of joy and bliss,
For each brings charms the others miss.

There Will Always Be Something to Do

There will always be something to do, my boy;
  There will always be wrongs to right;
There will always be need for a manly breed
  And men unafraid to fight.
There will always be honor to guard, my boy;
  There will always be hills to climb,
And tasks to do, and battles new
  From now to the end of time.

There will always be dangers to face, my boy;
  There will always be goals to take;
Men shall be tried, when the roads divide,
  And proved by the choice they make.
There will always be burdens to bear, my boy;
  There will always be need to pray;
There will always be tears through the future
      years,
  As loved ones are borne away.

There will always be God to serve, my boy,
  And always the Flag above;
They shall call to you until life is through
  For courage and strength and love.
So these are things that I dream, my boy,
  And have dreamed since your life began:
That whatever befalls, when the old world calls,
  It shall find you a sturdy man.

A Boy at Christmas

If I could have my wish to-night it would not be
    for wealth or fame,
It would not be for some delight that men who
    live in luxury claim,
But it would be that I might rise at three or four
    a. m. to see,
With eager, happy, boyish eyes, my presents on
    the Christmas tree.
Throughout this world there is no joy, I know
    now I am growing gray,
So rich as being just a boy, a little boy on Christ-
    mas Day.

I'd like once more to stand and gaze enraptured
    on a tinseled tree,
With eyes that know just how to blaze, a heart
    still tuned to ecstasy;
I'd like to feel the old delight, the surging thrills
    within me come;
To love a thing with all my might, to grasp the
    pleasure of a drum;
To know the meaning of a toy — a meaning lost
    to minds blasé;
To be just once again a boy, a little boy on Christ-
    mas Day.

I'd like to see a pair of skates the way they looked
    to me back then,

Before I'd turned from boyhood's gates and
      marched into the world of men;
I'd like to see a jackknife, too, with those same
      eager, dancing eyes
That couldn't fault or blemish view; I'd like to
      feel the same surprise,
The pleasure, free from all alloy, that has forever
      passed away,
When I was just a little boy and had my faith in
      Christmas Day.

Oh, little, laughing, roguish lad, the king that
      rules across the sea
Would give his scepter if he had such joy as now
      belongs to thee!
And beards of gray would give their gold, and
      all the honors they possess,
Once more within their grasp to hold thy present
      fee of happiness.
Earth sends no greater, surer joy, as, too soon,
      thou, as I, shall say,
Than that of him who is a boy, a little boy on
      Christmas Day.

Best Way to Read a Book

Best way to read a book I know
Is get a lad of six or so,
And curl him up upon my knee
Deep in a big arm chair, where we
Can catch the warmth of blazing coals,
And then let two contented souls
Melt into one, old age and youth,
Sharing adventure's marvelous truth.

I read a page, and then we sit
And talk it over, bit by bit;
Just how the pirates looked, and why
They flung a black flag to the sky.
We pass no paragraph without
First knowing what it's all about,
And when the author starts a fight
We join the forces that are right.

We're deep in Treasure Island, and
From Spy Glass Hill we've viewed the land;
Through thickets dense we've followed Jim
And shared the doubts that came to him.
We've heard Cap. Smollett arguing there
With Long John Silver, gaunt and spare,
And mastering our many fears
We've battled with those buccaneers.

Best way to read a book I've found
Is have a little boy around
And take him up upon your knee;
Then talk about the tale, till he
Lives it and feels it, just as you,
And shares the great adventure, too.
Books have a deep and lasting joy
For him who reads them to his boy.

The Song of Loved Ones

The father toils at his work all day,
And he hums this song as he plods away:
  "Heigho! for the mother and babe of three
  Who watch at the window each night for me.
  Their smiles are ever before my eyes,
  And never the sound of their voices dies,
  But ever and ever they seem to say,
  'Love waits for you at the close of day.'"

At home, a mother is heard to croon
To a little babe, this simple tune:
  "Heigho! for the father who toils to-day,
  He thinks of us, though he's far away;
  He soon will come with a happy tread,
  And stooping over your trundle bed,
  Your little worries he'll kiss away;
  Love comes to us at the close of day."

Becoming a Dad

Old women say that men don't know
The pain through which all mothers go,
And maybe that is true, and yet
I vow I never shall forget
The night he came. I suffered, too,
Those bleak and dreary long hours through;
I paced the floor and mopped my brow
And waited for his glad wee-ow!
I went upstairs and then came down,
Because I saw the doctor frown
And knew beyond the slightest doubt
He wished to goodness I'd clear out.

I walked into the yard for air
And back again to hear her there,
And met the nurse, as calm as though
My world was not in deepest woe,
And when I questioned, seeking speech
Of consolation that would reach
Into my soul and strengthen me
For dreary hours that were to be:
" Progressing nicely! " that was all
She said and tip-toed down the hall;
" Progressing nicely! " nothing more,
And left me there to pace the floor.

And once the nurse came out in haste
For something that had been misplaced,

And I that had been growing bold
Then felt my blood grow icy cold;
And fear's stern chill swept over me.
I stood and watched and tried to see
Just what it was she came to get.
I haven't learned that secret yet.
I half-believe that nurse in white
Was adding fuel to my fright
And taking an unholy glee,
From time to time, in torturing me.

Then silence! To her room I crept
And was informed the doctor slept!
The doctor slept! Oh, vicious thought,
While she at death's door bravely fought
And suffered untold anguish deep,
The doctor lulled himself to sleep.
I looked and saw him stretched out flat
And could have killed the man for that.
Then morning broke, and oh, the joy;
With dawn there came to us our boy,
And in a glorious little while
I went in there and saw her smile!

I must have looked a human wreck,
My collar wilted at the neck,
My hair awry, my features drawn
With all the suffering I had borne.
She looked at me and softly said,

"If I were you, I'd go to bed."
Her's was the bitterer part, I know;
She traveled through the vale of woe,
But now when women folks recall
The pain and anguish of it all
I answer them in manner sad:
"It's no cinch to become a dad."

The Test

You can brag about the famous men you know;
   You may boast about the great men you have
      met,
Parsons, eloquent and wise; stars in histrionic
      skies;
   Millionaires and navy admirals, and yet
Fame and power and wealth and glory vanish
      fast;
   They are lusters that were never made to
      stick,
And the friends worth-while and true, are the
      happy smiling few
   Who come to call upon you when you're sick.

You may think it very fine to know the great;
   You may glory in some leader's words of
      praise;
You may tell with eyes aglow of the public men
      you know,

But the true friends seldom travel glory's
    ways,
And the day you're lying ill, lonely, pale and
    keeping still,
    With a feverea pulse, that's beating double
        quick,
Then it is you must depend on the old-familiar
    friend
    To come to call upon you when you're sick.

It is pleasing to receive a great man's nod,
    And it's good to know the big men of the land,
But the test of friendship true, isn't merely:
    " Howdy-do? "
    And a willingness to shake you by the hand.
If you want to know the friends who love you
    best,
    And the faithful from the doubtful you would
        pick,
It is not a mighty task; of yourself you've but
    to ask:
    " Does he come to call upon me when I'm
        sick? "

The Old Wooden Tub

I like to get to thinking of the old days that are
      gone,
When there were joys that never more the world
      will look upon,
The days before inventors smoothed the little
      cares away
And made, what seemed but luxuries then, the
      joys of every day;
When bathrooms were exceptions, and we got
      our weekly scrub
By standing in the middle of a little wooden
      tub.

We had no rapid heaters, and no blazing gas to
      burn,
We boiled the water on the stove, and each one
      took his turn.
Sometimes to save expenses we would use one
      tub for two;
The water brother Billy used for me would
      also do,
Although an extra kettle I was granted, I admit,
On winter nights to freshen and to warm it up
      a bit.

We carried water up the stairs in buckets and
      in pails,

And sometimes splashed it on our legs, and rent
the air with wails,
But if the nights were very cold, by closing every
door
We were allowed to take our bath upon the
kitchen floor.
Beside the cheery stove we stood and gave ourselves a rub,
In comfort most luxurious in that old wooden
tub.

But modern homes no more go through that joyous weekly fun,
And through the sitting rooms at night no half-
dried children run;
No little flying forms go past, too swift to see
their charms,
With shirts and underwear and things tucked
underneath their arms;
The home's so full of luxury now, it's almost like
a club,
I sometimes wish we could go back to that old
wooden tub.

Lost Opportunities

"When I am rich," he used to say,
"A thousand joys I'll give away;
I'll walk among the poor I find
And unto one and all be kind.
I'll place a wreath of roses red
Upon the bier of all my dead;
I'll help the struggling youth to climb;
In doing good I'll spend my time;
To all in need I'll friendly be
The day that fortune smiles on me."

He never guessed that being kind
Depends upon the heart and mind
And not upon the purse at all;
That poor men's gifts, however small,
Make light some weary traveler's load
And smooth for him his troubled road.
He never knew or understood
The fellowship of doing good.
Because he had not much to spare
He thought it vain to give his share.

Yet many passed him, day by day,
He might have helped along the way.
He fancied kindness something which
Belongs entirely to the rich.
And so he lived and toiled for gold,

Unsympathetic, harsh and cold,
Intending all the time to share
The burdens that his brothers bear
When he possessed great wealth, and he
Could well afford a friend to be.

His fortune came, but, oh, too late;
The poor about him could not wait.
They never guessed and never knew
The things that he had meant to do.
Few knew how much he'd planned to give
If God had only let him live.
And when at last his form was cold,
All that he'd left on earth was gold.
A kindly name is something which
A man must earn before he's rich.

Patriotism

I think my country needs my vote,
I know it doesn't need my throat,
    My lungs and larynx, too;
And so I sit at home at night
And teach my children what is right
    And wise for them to do;
And when I'm on the job by day
I do my best to earn my pay.

Though arguments may rage and roar;
I grease the hinges on my door
    And paint the porches blue;
I love this splendid land of ours,
And so I plant the seeds and flowers
    And watch them bursting through.
I never stand upon a box
To say we're headed for the rocks.

My notion of a patriot
Is one who guards his little cot,
    And keeps it up to date;
Who pays his taxes when they're due,
And pays his bills for groc'ries, too,
    And dresses well his mate;
He keeps his children warmly clad
And lets them know they have a dad.

The nation's safe as long as men
Get to their work and back again
    Each day with cheerful smile;
So long as there are fathers who
Rejoice in what they have to do
    And find their homes worth while,
The Stars and Stripes will wave on high
And liberty will never die.

The Tramp

Eagerly he took my dime,
  Then shuffled on his way,
Thick with sin and filth and grime,
  But I wondered all that day
  How the man had gone astray.

Not to him the dime I gave;
  Not unto the man of woe,
Not to him who should be brave,
  Not to him who'd sunk so low,
  But the boy of long ago.

Passed his years of sin and shame
  Through the filth that all could see,
Out of what he is there came
  One more pitiful to me:
  Came the boy that used to be.

Smiling, full of promise glad,
  Stood a baby, like my own;
I beheld a glorious lad,
  Someone once had loved and known
  Out of which this wreck had grown!

Where, thought I, must lie the blame?
  Who has failed in such a way?
As all children come he came,
  There's a soul within his clay;
  Who has led his feet astray?

As he shuffled down the hall
  With the coin I'd never miss,
What, thought I, were fame and all
  Man may gain of earthly bliss,
  If my child should come to this!

The Lonely Garden

I wonder what the trees will say,
The trees that used to share his play,
An' knew him as the little lad
Who used to wander with his dad.
They've watched him grow from year to year
Since first the good Lord sent him here.
This shag-bark hick'ry, many a time,
The little fellow tried t' climb,
An' never a spring has come but he
Has called upon his favorite tree.
I wonder what they all will say
When they are told he's marched away.

I wonder what the birds will say,
The swallow an' the chatterin' jay,
The robin, an' the kill-deer, too.
For every one o' them, he knew,
An' every one o' them knew him,
An' hoppin' there from limb t' limb,
Waited each spring t' tell him all
They'd done an' seen since 'way last fall.
He was the first to greet 'em here
As they returned from year t' year;
An' now I wonder what they'll say
When they are told he's marched away.

I wonder how the roses there
Will get along without his care,
An' how the lilac bush will face
The loneliness about th' place;
For ev'ry spring an' summer, he
Has been the chum o' plant an' tree,
An' every livin' thing has known
A comradeship that's finer grown,
By havin' him from year t' year.
Now very soon they'll all be here,
An' I am wonderin' what they'll say
When they find out he's marched away.

The Silver Stripes

When we've honored the heroes returning from
France
And we've mourned for the heroes who fell,
When we've done all we can for the home-
coming man
Who stood to the shot and the shell,
Let us all keep in mind those who lingered
behind —
The thousands who waited to go —
The brave and the true, who did all they could do,
Yet have only the silver to show.

They went from their homes at the summons
for men,
They drilled in the heat of the sun,
They fell into line with a pluck that was fine;
Each cheerfully shouldered a gun.
They were ready to die for Old Glory on high,
They were eager to meet with the foe;
They were just like the rest of our bravest and
best,
Though they've only the silver to show.

Their bodies stayed here, but their spirits were
there;
And the boys who looked death in the face,

For the cause had no fear — for they knew,
        waiting here,
    There were many to fill up each place.
Oh, the ships came and went, till the battle was
        spent
    And the tyrant went down with the blow!
But he still might have reigned but for those who
        remained
    And have only the silver to show.

So here's to the soldiers who never saw France,
    And here's to the boys unafraid!
Let us give them their due; they were glorious,
        too,
    And it isn't their fault that they stayed.
They were eager to share in the sacrifice there;
    Let them share in the peace that we know.
For we know they were brave, by the service
        they gave,
    Though they've only the silver to show.

Tinkerin' at Home

Some folks there be who seem to need excitement
    fast and furious,
An' reckon all the joys that have no thrill in 'em
    are spurious.
Some think that pleasure's only found down
    where the lights are shining,
An' where an orchestra's at work the while the
    folks are dining.
Still others seek it at their play, while some there
    are who roam,
But I am happiest when I am tinkerin' 'round the
    home.

I like to wear my oldest clothes, an' fuss around
    the yard,
An' dig a flower bed now an' then, and pensively
    regard
The mornin' glories climbin' all along the wooden
    fence,
An' do the little odds an' ends that aren't of
    consequence.
I like to trim the hedges, an' touch up the paint
    a bit,
An' sort of take a homely pride in keepin' all
    things fit.
An' I don't envy rich folks who are sailin' o'er
    the foam

When I can spend a day or two in tinkerin'
    'round the home.

If I were fixed with money, as some other people
    are,
I'd take things mighty easy; I'd not travel very
    far.
I'd jes' wear my oldest trousers an' my flannel
    shirt, an' stay
An' guard my vine an' fig tree in an old man's
    tender way.
I'd bathe my soul in sunshine every mornin',
    and I'd bend
My back to pick the roses; Oh, I'd be a watchful
    friend
To everything around the place, an' in the twi-
    light gloam
I'd thank the Lord for lettin' me jes' tinker
    'round the home.

But since I've got to hustle in the turmoil of the
    town,
An' don't expect I'll ever be allowed to settle
    down
An' live among the roses an' the tulips an' the
    phlox,
Or spend my time in carin' for the noddin' holly-
    hocks,

I've come to the conclusion that perhaps in
     Heaven I may
Get a chance to know the pleasures that I'm
     yearnin' for to-day;
An' I'm goin' to ask the good Lord, when I've
     climbed the golden stair,
If he'll kindly let me tinker 'round the home we've
     got up there.

When An Old Man Gets to Thinking

When an old man gets to thinking of the years
     he's traveled through,
He hears again the laughter of the little ones he
     knew.
He isn't counting money, and he isn't planning
     schemes;
He's at home with friendly people in the shadow
     of his dreams.

When he's lived through all life's trials and his
     sun is in the west,
When he's tasted all life's pleasures and he knows
     which ones were best,
Then his mind is stored with riches, not of silver
     and of gold,
But of happy smiling faces and the joys he
     couldn't hold.

Could we see what he is seeing as he's dreaming
in his chair,
We should find no scene of struggle in the distance over there.
As he counts his memory treasures, we should see
some shady lane
Where's he walking with his sweetheart, young,
and arm in arm again.

We should meet with friendly people, simple,
tender folk and kind,
That had once been glad to love him. In his
dreaming we should find
All the many little beauties that enrich the lives
of men
That the eyes of youth scarce notice and the
poets seldom pen.

Age will tell you that the memory is the treasure-
house of man.
Gold and fleeting fame may vanish, but life's
riches never can;
For the little home of laughter and the voice of
every friend
And the joys of real contentment linger with us
to the end.

My Job

I wonder where's a better job than buying cake
    and meat,
And chocolate drops and sugar buns for little
    folks to eat?
And who has every day to face a finer round of
    care
Than buying frills and furbelows for little folks
    to wear?

Oh, you may brag how much you know and boast
    of what you do,
And think an all-important post has been assigned
    to you,
But I've the greatest job on earth, a task I'll
    never lose;
I've several pairs of little feet to keep equipped
    with shoes.

I rather like the job I have, though humble it
    may be,
And little gold or little fame may come from it
    to me;
It seems to me that life can give to man no finer
    joy
Than buying little breeches for a sturdy little
    boy.

My job is not to run the world or pile up bonds
    and stocks;
It's just to keep two little girls in plain and fancy
    frocks;
To dress and feed a growing boy whose legs are
    brown and stout,
And furnish stockings just as fast as he can
    wear them out.

I would not for his crown and throne change
    places with a king,
I've got the finest job on earth and unto it I'll
    cling;
I know no better task than mine, no greater
    chance for joys,
Than serving day by day the needs of little girls
    and boys.

A Good Name

Men talk too much of gold and fame,
And not enough about a name;
And yet a good name's better far
Than all earth's glistening jewels are.
Who holds his name above all price
And chooses every sacrifice
To keep his earthly record clear,
Can face the world without a fear.

Who never cheats nor lies for gain,
A poor man may, perhaps, remain,
Yet, when at night he goes to rest,
No little voice within his breast
Disturbs his slumber. Conscience clear,
He falls asleep with naught to fear
And when he wakes the world to face
He is not tainted by disgrace.

Who keeps his name without a stain
Wears no man's brand and no man's chain;
He need not fear to speak his mind
In dread of what the world may find.
He then is master of his will;
None may command him to be still,
Nor force him, when he would stand fast,
To flinch before his hidden past.

Not all the gold that men may claim
Can cover up a deed of shame;
Not all the fame of victory sweet
Can free the man who played the cheat;
He lives a slave unto the last
Unto the shame that mars his past.
He only freedom here may own
Whose name a stain has never known.

Alone

Strange thoughts come to the man alone;
  'Tis then, if ever, he talks with God,
  And views himself as a single clod
In the soil of life where the souls are grown.
'Tis then he questions the why and where,
  The start and end of his years and days,
  And what is blame and what is praise,
And what is ugly and what is fair.

When a man has drawn from the busy throng
  To the sweet retreat of the silent hours,
  Low voices whisper of higher powers.
He catches the strain of some far-off song,
And the sham fades out and his eyes can see,
  Not the man he is in the day's hot strife
  And the greed and grind of a selfish life,
But the soul of the man he is to be.

He feels the throbbing of life divine,
  And catches a glimpse of the greater plan;
  He questions the purpose and work of man.
In the hours of silence his mind grows fine;
He seeks to learn what is kept unknown;
  He turns from self and its garb of clay
  And dwells on the soul and the higher way.
Strange thoughts come when a man's alone.

Shut-Ins

We're gittin' so we need again
To see the sproutin' seed again.
We've been shut up all winter long
Within our narrow rooms;
We're sort o' shriveled up an' dry —
Ma's cranky-like an' quick to cry;
We need the blue skies overhead,
The garden with its blooms.

I'm findin' fault with this an' that!
I threw my bootjack at the cat
Because he rubbed against my leg —
I guess I'm all on edge;
I'm fidgety an' fussy too,
An' Ma finds fault with all I do;
It seems we need to see again
The green upon the hedge.

We've been shut up so long, it seems
We've lost the glamour of our dreams.
We've narrowed down as people will
Till fault is all we see.
We need to stretch our souls in air
Where there is room enough to spare;
We need the sight o' something green
On every shrub an' tree.

But soon our petulance will pass —
Our feet will tread the dew-kissed grass;
Our souls will break their narrow cells,
An' swell with love once more.
And with the blue skies overhead,
The harsh an' hasty words we've said
Will vanish with the snow an' ice,
When spring unlocks the door.

The sun will make us sweet again
With blossoms at our feet again;
We'll wander, arm in arm, the ways
Where beauty reigns supreme.
An' Ma an' I shall smile again,
An' be ourselves awhile again,
An' claim, like prisoners set free,
The charm of every dream.

The Cut-Down Trousers

When father couldn't wear them mother cut them
    down for me;
He took the slack in fore and aft, and hemmed
    them at the knee;
They fitted rather loosely, but the things that
    made me glad
Were the horizontal pockets that those good old
    trousers had.

They shone like patent leather just where we[ll]
    worn breeches do,
But the cloth in certain portions was consider[e]
    good as new,
And I know that I was envied by full many [a]
    richer lad
For the horizontal pockets that those good o[ld]
    knickers had.

They were cut along the waist line, with the ope[n]
    ing straight and wide,
And there wasn't any limit to what you could g[et]
    inside;
They would hold a peck of marbles, and a kni[fe]
    and top and string,
And snakes and frogs and turtles; there was roo[m]
    for everything.

Then our fortune changed a little, and my moth[er]
    said that she
Wouldn't bother any longer fitting father's du[ds]
    on me,
But the store clothes didn't please me; there we[re]
    times they made me sad,
For I missed those good old pockets that m[y]
    father's trousers had.

Dinner-Time

Tuggin' at your bottle,
  An' it's O, you're mighty sweet!
Just a bunch of dimples
  From your top-knot to your feet,
Lying there an' gooin'
  In the happiest sort o' way,
Like a rosebud peekin' at me
  In the early hours o' day;
Gloating over goodness
  That you know an' sense an' clutch,
An' smilin' at your daddy,
  Who loves you, O, so much!

Tuggin' at your bottle,
  As you nestle in your crib,
With your daddy grinnin' at you
  'Cause you've dribbled on your bib,
An' you gurgle an' you chortle
  Like a brook in early Spring;
An' you kick your pink feet gayly,
  An' I think you'd like to sing.
All you wanted was your dinner,
  Daddy knew it too, you bet!
An' the moment that you got it
  Then you ceased to fuss an' fret.

Tuggin' at your bottle,
  Not a care, excepting when

You lose the rubber nipple,
  But you find it soon again;
An' the gurglin' an' the gooin'
  An' the chortlin' start anew,
An' the kickin' an' the squirmin'
  Show the wondrous joy o' you.
But I'll bet you're not as happy
  At your dinner, little tot,
As the weather-beaten daddy
  Who is bendin' o'er your cot!

The Pay Envelope

Is it all in the envelope holding your pay?
Is that all you're working for day after day?
Are you getting no more from your toil than
    the gold
That little enclosure of paper will hold?
Is that all you're after; is that all you seek?
Does that close the deal at the end of the week?

Is it all in the envelope holding his pay?
Is that all you offer him day after day?
Is that all he wins by his labor from you?
Is that the reward for the best he can do?
Would you say of your men, when the week has
    been turned,

That all they've received is the money they've
    earned?

Is it all in the envelope, workman and chief?
Then loyalty's days must be fleeting and brief;
If you measure your work by its value in gold
The sum of your worth by your pay shall be told;
And if something of friendship your men do not
    find
Outside of their envelopes, you're the wrong kind.

If all that you offer is silver and gold,
You haven't a man in your plant you can hold.
If all that you're after each week is your pay,
You are doing your work in a short-sighted way:
For the bigger rewards it is useless to hope
If you never can see past the pay envelope.

The Evening Prayer

Little girlie, kneeling there,
Speaking low your evening prayer,
In your cunning little nightie
With your pink toes peeping through,
With your eyes closed and your hands
Tightly clasped, while daddy stands
In the doorway, just to hear the
"God bless papa," lisped by you,
You don't know just what I feel,
As I watch you nightly kneel
By your trundle bed and whisper
Soft and low your little prayer!
But in all I do or plan,
I'm a bigger, better man
Every time I hear you asking
God to make my journey fair.

Little girlie, kneeling there,
Lisping low your evening prayer,
Asking God above to bless me
At the closing of each day,
Oft the tears come to my eyes,
And I feel a big lump rise
In my throat, that I can't swallow,
And I sometimes turn away.
In the morning, when I wake,
And my post of duty take,

I go forth with new-born courage
To accomplish what is fair;
And, throughout the live-long day,
I am striving every way
To come back to you each evening
And be worthy of your prayer.

Thoughts of a Father

We've never seen the Father here, but we have
    known the Son,
The finest type of manhood since the world was
    first begun.
And, summing up the works of God, I write with
    reverent pen,
The greatest is the Son He sent to cheer the lives
    of men.

Through Him we learned the ways of God and
    found the Father's love;
The Son it was who won us back to Him who
    reigns above.
The Lord did not come down himself to prove
    to men His worth,
He sought our worship through the Child He
    placed upon the earth.

How can I best express my life? Wherein does
    greatness lie?
How can I long remembrance win, since I am
    born to die?
Both fame and gold are selfish things; their
    charms may quickly flee,
But I'm the father of a boy who came to speak
    for me.

In him lies all I hope to be; his splendor shall be
    mine;
I shall have done man's greatest work if only
    he is fine.
If some day he shall help the world long after
    I am dead,
In all that men shall say of him my praises shall
    be said.

It matters not what I may win of fleeting gold
    or fame,
My hope of joy depends alone on what my boy
    shall claim.
My story must be told through him, for him I
    work and plan,
Man's greatest duty is to be the father of a man.

When a Little Baby Dies

When a little baby dies
And its wee form silent lies,
And its little cheeks seem waxen
And its little hands are still,
Then your soul gives way to treason,
And you cry: " O, God, what reason,
O, what justice and what mercy
Have You shown us by Your will?

"There are, O, so many here
Of the yellow leaf and sere,
Who are anxious, aye, and ready
To respond unto Your call;
Yet You pass them by unheeding,
And You set our hearts to bleeding!
" O," you mutter, " God, how cruel
Do Your vaunted mercies fall! "

Yet some day, in after years,
When Death's angel once more nears,
And the unknown, silent river
Looms as darkly as a pall,
You will hear your baby saying,
" Mamma, come to me, I'm staying
With my arms outstretched to greet you,"
And you'll understand it all.

To the Boy

I have no wish, my little lad,
   To climb the towering heights of fame.
I am content to be your dad
   And share with you each pleasant game.
I am content to hold your hand
   And walk along life's path with you,
And talk of things we understand —
   The birds and trees and skies of blue.

Though some may seek the smiles of kings,
   For me your laughter's joy enough;
I have no wish to claim the things
   Which lure men into pathways rough.
I'm happiest when you and I,
   Unmindful of life's bitter cares,
Together watch the clouds drift by,
   Or follow boyhood's thoroughfares.

I crave no more of life than this:
   Continuance of such a trust;
Your smile, whate'er the morning is,
   Until my clay returns to dust.
If but this comradeship may last
   Until I end my earthly task —
Your hand and mine by love held fast —
   Fame has no charm for which I'd ask.

I would not trade one day with you
    To wear the purple robes of power,
Nor drop your hand from mine to do
    Some great deed in a selfish hour.
For you have brought me joy serene
    And made my soul supremely glad.
In life rewarded I have been;
    'Twas all worth while to be your dad.

His Dog

Pete bristles when the doorbell rings.
    Last night he didn't act the same.
Dogs have a way of knowin' things,
    An' when the dreaded cable came,
He looked at mother an' he whined
    His soft, low sign of somethin' wrong,
As though he knew that we should find
    The news that we had feared so long.

He's followed me about the place
    An' hasn't left my heels to-day;
He's rubbed his nose against my face
    As if to kiss my grief away.
There on his plate beside the door
    You'll see untouched his mornin' meal.
I never understood before
    That dogs share every hurt you feel.

We've got the pride o' service fine
  As consolation for the blow;
We know by many a written line
  He went the way he wished to go.
We know that God an' Country found
  Our boy a servant brave an' true —
But Pete must sadly walk around
  An' miss the master that he knew.

The mother's bearing up as well
  As such a noble mother would;
The hurt I feel I needn't tell —
  I guess by all it's understood.
But Pete — his dog — that used to wait
  Each night to hear his cheery call,
An' romped about him at the gate,
  Has felt the blow the worst of all.

Lullaby

The golden dreamboat's ready, all her silken sails
    are spread,
And the breeze is gently blowing to the fairy
    port of Bed,
And the fairy's captain's waiting while the busy
    sandman flies
With the silver dust of slumber, closing every
    baby's eyes.

Oh, the night is rich with moonlight and the sea
  is calm with peace,
And the angels fly to guard you and their watch
  shall never cease,
And the fairies there await you; they have splendid dreams to spin;
You shall hear them gayly singing as the dreamboat's putting in.

Like the ripple of the water does the dreamboat's
  whistle blow,
Only baby ears can catch it when it comes the
  time to go,
Only little ones may journey on so wonderful a
  ship,
And go drifting off to slumber with no care to
  mar the trip.

Oh, the little eyes are heavy but the little soul is
  light;
It shall never know a sorrow or a terror through
  the night.
And at last when dawn is breaking and the
  dreamboat's trip is o'er,
You shall wake to find the mother smiling over
  you once more.

The Old-Fashioned Parents

The good old-fashioned mothers and the good
    old-fashioned dads,
With their good old-fashioned lassies and their
    good old-fashioned lads,
Still walk the lanes of loving in their simple,
    tender ways,
As they used to do back yonder in the good old-
    fashioned days.

They dwell in every city and they live in every
    town,
Contentedly and happy and not hungry for
    renown;
On every street you'll find 'em in their simple
    garments clad,
The good old-fashioned mother and the good
    old-fashioned dad.

There are some who sigh for riches, there are
    some who yearn for fame,
And a few misguided people who no longer blush
    at shame;
But the world is full of mothers, and the world is
    full of dads,
Who are making sacrifices for their little girls
    and lads.

They are growing old together, arm in arm they
      walk along,
And their hearts with love are beating and their
      voices sweet with song;
They still share their disappointments and they
      share their pleasures, too,
And whatever be their fortune, to each other
      they are true.

They are watching at the bedside of a baby pale
      and white,
And they kneel and pray together for the care
      of God at night;
They are romping with their children in the fields
      of clover sweet,
And devotedly they guard them from the perils
      of the street.

They are here in countless numbers, just as they
      have always been,
And their glory is untainted by the selfish and
      the mean.
And I'd hate to still be living, it would dismal be
      and sad,
If we'd no old-fashioned mother and we'd no
      old-fashioned dad.

The Fun of Forgiving

Sometimes I'm almost glad to hear when I g[e]
    home that they've been bad;
And though I try to look severe, within my hea[rt]
    I'm really glad
When mother sadly tells to me the list of awf[ul]
    things they've done,
Because when they come tearfully, forgivin[g]
    them is so much fun.

I like to have them all alone, with no one nea[r]
    to hear or see,
Then as their little faults they own, I like to tak[e]
    them on my knee
And talk it over and pretend the whipping soo[n]
    must be begun;
And then to kiss them at the end — forgivin[g]
    them is so much fun.

Within the world there's no such charm as chi[l]
    dren penitent and sad,
Who put two soft and chubby arms around you[r]
    neck, when they've been bad.
And as you view their trembling lips, away you[r]
    temper starts to run,
And from your mind all anger slips — forgivin[g]
    them is so much fun.

If there were nothing to forgive I wonder if
    we'd love them so;
If they were wise enough to live as grown-ups
    do, and always go
Along the pleasant path of right, with ne'er a
    fault from sun to sun,
A lot of joys we'd miss at night — forgiving
    them is so much fun.

Tonsils

One day the doctor came because my throat was
    feeling awful sore,
And when he looked inside to see he said: " It's
    like it was before;
It's tonserlitis, sure enough. You'd better tell
    her Pa to-day
To make his mind up now to have that little
    party right away."

I'd heard him talk that way before when Bud
    was sick, and so I knew
That what they did to him that time, to me they
    planned to come and do.
An' when my Pa came home that night Ma said:
    " She can't grow strong and stout
Until the doctor comes an' takes her addynoids
    an' tonsils out."

163

An' then Pa took me on his knee and kissed me
    solemn-like an' grave,
An' said he guessed it was the best, an' then he
    asked me to be brave.
Ma said: "Don't look at her like that, it's
    nothing to be scared about";
An Pa said: "True, but still I wish she needn't
    have her tonsils out."

Next morning when I woke, Ma said I couldn't
    have my breakfast then,
Because the doctors and the nurse had said they
    would be here by ten.
When they got here the doctor smiled an' gave
    me some perfume to smell,
An' told me not to cry at all, coz pretty soon
    I would be well.

When I woke up Ma smiled an' said: "It's all
    right now"; but in my head
It seemed like wheels were buzzing round and
    everywhere I looked was red.
An' I can't eat hard cookies yet, nor use my
    voice at all to shout,
But Pa an' Ma seem awful glad that I have had
    my tonsils out.

At Dawn

hey come to my room at the break of the day,
With their faces all smiles and their minds full
    of play;
hey come on their tip-toes and silently creep
o the edge of the bed where I'm lying asleep,
nd then at a signal, on which they agree,
With a shout of delight they jump right onto me.

hey lift up my eyelids and tickle my nose,
nd scratch at my cheeks with their little pink
    toes;
nd sometimes to give them a laugh and a scare
snap and I growl like a cinnamon bear;
hen over I roll, and with three kids astride
gallop away on their feather-bed ride.

've thought it all over. Man's biggest mistake
s in wanting to sleep when his babes are awake;
When they come to his room for that first bit of
    fun
Ie should make up his mind that his sleeping is
    done;
Ie should share in the laughter they bring to his
    side
nd start off the day with that feather-bed ride.

)h they're fun at their breakfast and fun at their
    lunch;

Any hour of the day they're a glorious bunch!
When they're togged up for Sundays they're ce:
    tainly fine,
And I'm glad in my heart I can call them all min
But I think that the time that I like them the be:
Is that hour in the morning before they a:
    dressed.

Names and Faces

I do not ask a store of wealth,
    Nor special gift of power;
I hope always for strength and health
    To brave each troubled hour.
But life would be distinctly good,
    However low my place is,
Had I a memory that could
    Remember names and faces.

I am not troubled by the fact
    That common skill is mine;
I care not that my life has lacked
    The glory of the fine.
But, oh, when someone speaks to me,
    My cheeks grow red with shame
Because I'm sure that he must see
    That I have lost his name.

Embarrassment, where'er I go,
    Pursues me night and day;
I hear some good friend's glad " Hello,"
    And stop a word to say.
His voice melodiously may ring,
    But that's all lost on me,
For all the time I'm wondering
    Whoever can he be.

I envy no man's talent rare
    Save his who can repeat
The names of men, no matter where
    It is they chance to meet.
For he escapes the bitter blow,
    The sorrow and regret,
Of greeting friends he ought to know
    As though they'd never met.

I do not ask a store of gold,
    High station here, or fame;
I have no burning wish to hold
    The popular acclaim;
Life's lanes I'd gladly journey through,
    Nor mind the stony places,
Could I but do as others do
    And know men's names and faces!

Pleasing Dad

When I was but a little lad, not more than two or
        three,
I noticed in a general way my dad was proud of
        me.
He liked the little ways I had, the simple things
        I said;
Sometimes he gave me words of praise, sometimes
        he stroked my head;
And when I'd done a thing worth while, the
        thought that made me glad
Was always that I'd done my best, and that
        would please my dad.

I can look back to-day and see how proud he
        used to be
When I'd come home from school and say they'd
        recommended me.
I didn't understand it then, for school boys never
        do,
But in a vague and general way it seems to me
        I knew
That father took great pride in me, and wanted
        me to shine,
And that it meant a lot to him when I'd done
        something fine.

Then one day out of school I went, amid the
        great world's hum,

An office boy, and father watched each night to
    see me come.
And I recall how proud he was of me that
    wondrous day
When I could tell him that, unasked, the firm had
    raised my pay.
I still can feel that hug he gave, I understand the
    joy
It meant to him to learn that men were trusting
    in his boy.

I wonder will it please my dad? How oft the
    thought occurs
When I am stumbling on the paths, beset with
    briars and burrs!
He isn't here to see me now, alone my race I
    run,
And yet some day I'll go to him and tell him all
    I've done.
And oh I pray that when we meet beyond life's
    stormy sea
That he may claim the old-time joy of being
    proud of me.

Living Flowers

" I'm never alone in the garden," he said. " I'm
    never alone with the flowers.
It seems like I'm meeting the wonderful dead
    out here with these blossoms of ours.
An' there's never a bush or a plant or a tree, but
    somebody loved it of old.
An' the souls of the angels come talkin' to me
    through the petals of crimson an' gold.

" The lilacs in spring bring the mother once more,
    an' she lives in the midsummer rose.
She smiles in the peony clump at the door, an'
    sings when the four o'clocks close.
She loved every blossom God gave us to own, an'
    daily she gave it her care.
So never I walk in the garden alone, for I feel
    that the mother's still there.

" These are the pinks that a baby once kissed,
    still spicy with fragrance an' fair.
The years have been long since her laughter I've
    missed, but her spirit is hovering there.
The roses that ramble and twine on the wall were
    planted by one that was kind
An' I'm sure as I stand here an' gaze on them all,
    that his soul has still lingered behind.

"I'm never alone in the garden," he said, "I
    have many to talk with an' see,
For never a flower comes to bloom in its bed, but
    it brings back a loved one to me.
An' I fancy whenever I'm bendin' above these
    blossoms of crimson an' gold,
That I'm seein' an' hearin' the ones that I love,
    who lived in the glad days of old."

The Common Joys

These joys are free to all who live,
    The rich and poor, the great and low:
The charms which kindness has to give,
    The smiles which friendship may bestow,
The honor of a well-spent life,
    The glory of a purpose true,
High courage in the stress of strife,
    And peace when every task is through.

Nor class nor caste nor race nor creed,
    Nor greater might can take away
The splendor of an honest deed.
    Who nobly serves from day to day
Shall walk the road of life with pride,
    With friends who recognize his worth,
For never are these joys denied
    Unto the humblest man on earth.

Not all may rise to world-wide fame,
  Not all may gather fortune's gold,
Not all life's luxuries may claim;
  In differing ways success is told.
But all may know the peace of mind
  Which comes from service brave and true;
The poorest man can still be kind,
  And nobly live till life is through.

These joys abound for one and all:
  The pride of fearing no man's scorn,
Of standing firm, where others fall,
  Of bearing well what must be borne.
He that shall do an honest deed
  Shall win an honest deed's rewards;
For these, no matter race or creed,
  Life unto every man affords.

His Example

There are little eyes upon you, and they're watch-
      ing night and day;
There are little ears that quickly take in every
      word you say;
There are little hands all eager to do everything
      you do,
And a little boy that's dreaming of the day he'll
      be like you.

You're the little fellow's idol, you're the wisest
    of the wise;
In his little mind about you no suspicions ever
    rise;
He believes in you devoutly, holds that all you
    say and do
He will say and do in your way when he's grown
    up just like you.

Oh, it sometimes makes me shudder when I
    hear my boy repeat
Some careless phrase I've uttered in the language
    of the street;
And it sets my heart to grieving when some little
    fault I see
And I know beyond all doubting that he picked
    it up from me.

There's a wide-eyed little fellow who believes
    you're always right,
And his ears are always open and he watches
    day and night;
You are setting an example every day in all
    you do
For the little boy who's waiting to grow up to
    be like you.

The Change-Worker

A feller don't start in to think of himself, an'
    the part that he's playin' down here,
When there's nobody lookin' to him fer support,
    an' he don't give a thought to next year.
His faults don't seem big an' his habits no worse
    than a whole lot of others he knows,
An' he don't seem to care what his neighbors may
    say, as heedlessly forward he goes.
He don't stop to think if it's wrong or it's right;
    with his speech he is careless or glib,
Till the minute the nurse lets him into the room
    to see what's asleep in the crib.

An' then as he looks at that bundle o' red, an' the
    wee little fingers an' toes,
An' he knows it's his flesh an' his blood that is
    there, an' will be just like him when it
    grows,
It comes in a flash to a feller right then, there is
    more here than pleasure or pelf,
An' the sort of a man his baby will be is the sort
    of a man he's himself.
Then he kisses the mother an' kisses the child, an'
    goes out determined that he
Will endeavor to be just the sort of a man that
    he's wantin' his baby to be.

A feller don't think that it matters so much what
     he does till a baby arrives;
He sows his wild oats an' he has his gay fling an'
     headlong in pleasure he dives;
An' a drink more or less doesn't matter much
     then, for life is a comedy gay,
But the moment a crib is put in the home, an' a
     baby has come there to stay,
He thinks of the things he has done in the past,
     an' it strikes him as hard as a blow,
That the path he has trod in the past is a path
     that he don't want his baby to go.

I ain't much to preach, an' I can't just express
     in the way that your clever men can
The thoughts that I think, but it seems to me now
     that when God wants to rescue a man
From himself an' the follies that harmless ap-
     pear, but which, under the surface, are
     grim,
He summons the angel of infancy sweet, an' sends
     down a baby to him.
For in that way He opens his eyes to himself, and
     He gives him the vision to see
That his duty's to be just the sort of a man that
     he's wantin' his baby to be.

A Convalescin' Woman

A convalescin' woman does the strangest sort o'
    things,
An' it's wonderful the courage that a little new
    strength brings;
O, it's never safe to leave her for an hour or two
    alone,
Or you'll find th' doctor's good work has been
    quickly overthrown.
There's that wife o' mine, I reckon she's a sample
    of 'em all;
She's been mighty sick, I tell you, an' to-day can
    scarcely crawl,
But I left her jes' this mornin' while I fought
    potater bugs,
An' I got back home an' caught her in the back
    yard shakin' rugs.

I ain't often cross with Nellie, an' I let her have
    her way,
But it made me mad as thunder when I got back
    home to-day
An' found her doin' labor that'd tax a big man's
    strength;
An' I guess I lost my temper, for I scolded her
    at length,
'Til I seen her teardrops fallin' an' she said: "I
    couldn't stand

To see those rugs so dirty, so I took 'em all in
hand,
An' it ain't hurt me nuther — see, I'm gettin'
strong again — "
An' I said : " Doggone it ! can't ye leave sich
work as that fer men? "

Once I had her in a hospittle fer weeks an' weeks
an' weeks,
An' she wasted most to nothin', an' th' roses left
her cheeks;
An' one night I feared I'd lose her; 'twas the
turnin' point, I guess,
Coz th' next day I remember that th' doctor said :
" Success ! "

Well, I brought her home an' told her that for
two months she must stay
A-sittin' in her rocker an' jes' watch th' kids at
play.
An' th' first week she was patient, but I mind the
way I swore
On th' day when I discovered 'at she'd scrubbed
th' kitchen floor.

O, you can't keep wimmin quiet, an' they ain't
a bit like men;
They're hungerin' every minute jes' to get to
work again;

An' you've got to watch 'em allus, when yo▋
    know they're weak an' ill,
Coz th' minute that yer back is turned they'▋
    labor fit to kill.
Th' house ain't cleaned to suit 'em an' they seer▋
    to fret an' fume
'Less they're busy doin' somethin' with a mo▋
    or else a broom;
An' it ain't no use to scold 'em an' it ain't no us▋
    to swear,
Coz th' next time they will do it jes' the minut▋
    you ain't there.

The Doubtful To-Morrow

Whenever I walk through God's Acres of Dea▋
I wonder how often the mute voices said:
" I will do a kind deed or will lighten a sorrow
Or rise to a sacrifice splendid — to-morrow."

I wonder how many fine thoughts unexpressed
Were lost to the world when they went to the▋
       rest;
I wonder what beautiful deeds they'd have do▋
If they had but witnessed to-morrow's bright su▋

Oh, if the dead grieve, it is not for their fate,

'or death comes to all of us early or late,
;ut their sighs of regret and their burdens of
    sorrow
.re born of the joys they'd have scattered to-
    morrow.

'o the friends they'd have cheered know the
    thoughts of the dead?
'o they treasure to-day the last words that were
    said?
/hat mem'ries would sweeten, what hearts cease
    to burn,
' but for a day the dead friends could return!

'e know not the hour that our summons shall
    come;
'e know not the time that our voice shall be
    dumb,
et even as they, to our ultimate sorrow,
'e leave much that's fine for that doubtful
    to-morrow.

He was battle-scarred and ugly with the mark
    of shot and shell,
And we knew that British Tommy had a stirring
    tale to tell,
So we asked him where he got it and what dis-
    arranged his face,
And he answered, blushing scarlet: " In a nawsty
    little place "

There were medals on his jacket, but he wouldn't
    tell us why.
" A bit lucky, gettin' this one," was the sum of
    his reply.
He had fought a horde of Prussians with his
    back against the wall,
And he told us, when we questioned: " H'it
    was nothing arfter h'all."

Not a word of what he'd suffered, not a word
    of what he'd seen,
Not a word about the fury of the hell through
    which he'd been.
All he said was: " When you're cornered, h'an'
    you've got no plyce to go,
You've just got to stand up to it! You cawn't
    'elp yourself, you know.

"H'it was just a bit unpleasant, when the shells
        were droppin' thick,"
And he tapped his leather leggins with his little
        bamboo stick.
"What did H'I do? Nothing, really! Nothing
        more than just my share;
Some one h'else would gladly do it, but H'I 'ap-
        pened to be there."

When this sturdy British Tommy quits the battle-
        fields of earth
And St. Peter asks his spirit to recount his deeds
        of worth,
I fancy I can hear him, with his curious English
        drawl,
Saying: "Nothing, nothing really, that's worth
        mentioning at h'all."

The Right Family

With time our notions allus change,
An' years make old idees seem strange —
Take Mary there — time was when she
Thought one child made a family,
An' when our eldest, Jim, was born
She used to say, both night an' morn':
" One little one to love an' keep,
To guard awake, an' watch asleep;
To bring up right an' lead him through
Life's path is all we ought to do."

Two years from then our Jennie came,
But Mary didn't talk the same;
" Now that's just right," she said to me,
" We've got the proper family —
A boy an' girl, God sure is good;
It seems as though He understood
That I've been hopin' every way
To have a little girl some day;
Sometimes I've prayed the whole night through —
One ain't enough; we needed two."

Then as the months went rollin on,
One day the stork brought little John,
An' Mary smiled an' said to me;
" The proper family is three;
Two boys, a girl to romp an' play —

Jus' work enough to fill the day.
I never had enough to do,
The months that we had only two;
Three's jus' right, pa, we don't want more."
Still time went on an' we had four.

An' that was years ago, I vow,
An' we have six fine children now;
An' Mary's plumb forgot the day
She used to sit an' sweetly say
That one child was enough for her
To love an' give the proper care;
One, two or three or four or five —
Why, goodness gracious, sakes alive,
If God should send her ten to-night,
She'd vow her fam'ly was jus' right!

A Lesson from Golf

He couldn't use his driver any better on the tee
Than the chap that he was licking, who just
happened to be me;
I could hit them with a brassie just as straight
and just as far,
But I piled up several sevens while he made a
few in par;
And he trimmed me to a finish, and I know the
reason why:
He could keep his temper better when he dubbed
a shot than I.

His mashie stroke is choppy, without any follow
through;
I doubt if he will ever, on a short hole, cop a
two,
But his putts are straight and deadly, and he
doesn't even frown
When he's tried to hole a long one and just fails
to get it down.
On the fourteenth green I faded; there he put
me on the shelf,
And it's not to his discredit when I say I licked
myself.

He never whined or whimpered when a shot of
his went wrong;

Never kicked about his troubles, but just plodded
     right along.
When he flubbed an easy iron, though I knew
     that he was vexed,
He merely shrugged his shoulders, and then
     coolly played the next,
While I flew into a frenzy over every dub I
     made
And was loud in my complaining at the dismal
     game I played.

Golf is like the game of living; it will show up
     what you are;
If you take your troubles badly you will never
     play to par.
You may be a fine performer when your skies
     are bright and blue
But disaster is the acid that shall prove the worth
     of you;
So just meet your disappointments with a cheery
     sort of grin,
For the man who keeps his temper is the man
     that's sure to win.

Father's Chore

My Pa can hit his thumbnail with a hammer and
  keep still;
  He can cut himself while shaving an' not
  swear;
If a ladder slips beneath him an' he gets a nasty
  spill
  He can smile as though he really didn't care.
But the pan beneath the ice-box — when he goes
  to empty that —
  Then a sound-proof room the children have
  to hunt;
For we have a sad few minutes in our very
  pleasant flat
  When the water in it splashes down his front.

My Pa believes his temper should be all the time
  controlled;
  He doesn't rave at every little thing;
When his collar-button underneath the chiffonier
  has rolled
  A snatch of merry ragtime he will sing.
But the pan beneath the ice box — when to empty
  that he goes —
  As he stoops to drag it out we hear a grunt;
From the kitchen comes a rumble, an' then every-
  body knows
  That he splashed the water in it down his front.

Now the distance from the ice box to the sink's
    not very far —
  I'm sure it isn't over twenty feet —
But though very short the journey, it is long
    enough for Pa
  As he travels it disaster grim to meet.
And it's seldom that he makes it without accident,
    although
  In the summer time it is his nightly stunt;
And he says a lot of language that no gentleman
    should know
  When the water in it splashes down his front.

The March o' Man

Down to work o' mornings, an' back to home at
    nights,
Down to hours o' labor, an' home to sweet
    delights;
Down to care an' trouble, an' home to love an'
    rest,
With every day a good one, an' every evening
    blest.

Down to dreary dollars, an' back to home to play,
From love to work an' back to love, so slips the
    day away.
From babies back to business an' back to babes
    again,
From parting kiss to welcome kiss, this marks
    the march o' men.

Some care between our laughter, a few hours
    filled with strife,
A time to stand on duty, then home to babes
    and wife;
The bugle sounds o' mornings to call us to the
    fray,
But sweet an' low 'tis love that calls us home at
    close o' day.

INDEX OF FIRST LINES